VISIONS

AND

REVISIONS

VISIONS AND REVISIONS

An Approach to Poetry

Barry Wallenstein

The City College of the City University of New York

THOMAS Y. CROWELL COMPANY

NEW YORK   *Established 1834*

L. C. Card 70-136034
ISBN 0–690–86404–3
Manufactured in the United States of America

ACKNOWLEDGMENTS

Acknowledgment is gratefully made to the following authors and publishers for permission to reprint copyrighted material:

W. H. Auden, "Taller To-day," "Consider," and "No Change of Place," copyright © 1934, renewed 1962, by W. H. Auden; "A Summer Night," copyright © 1937 by Random House, Inc., renewed 1965 by W. H. Auden; "Herman Melville," and "In Memory of W. B. Yeats," copyright © 1940, renewed 1968, by W. H. Auden; "At the Grave of Henry James," copyright © 1941, renewed 1969, by W. H. Auden; "Through the Looking Glass," "Journey to Iceland," "Sonnets from China XXI (To E. M. Forster)," and "Hong Kong," copyright © 1945 by W. H. Auden, from Collected Shorter Poems, 1927–1957 (New York: Random House, Inc., 1967), reprinted by permission of Random House, Inc. and Faber and Faber Ltd.

Emily Dickinson, "Because that you are going" and "If those I loved were lost," copyright © 1951, 1955 by The President and Fellows of Harvard College, from Thomas H. Johnson, ed., The Poems of Emily Dickinson (Cambridge, Mass.: The Belknap Press of Harvard University Press, 1955), reprinted by permission of the publishers and the Trustees of Amherst College. "My life had stood—a loaded gun," copyright © 1929, 1957 by Mary L. Hampson, from Thomas H. Johnson, ed., The Complete Poems of Emily Dickinson (Boston: Little, Brown and Company, 1957), reprinted by permission of the publisher.

Horace Gregory, translator, Poem LVIII and Poem XCII, The Poems of Catullus (New York: Grove Press, Inc., 1956). Copyright © 1956 by Horace Gregory. Reprinted by permission of Grove Press, Inc.

D. H. Lawrence, "Piano," "Violets," and "Renaissance," copyright ©
1920 by B. W. Huebsch, Inc., renewed 1948 by Frieda Lawrence; "Man's
Image," copyright © 1929 by Frieda Lawrence Ravagli; "Bavarian Gen-
tians," copyright © 1933 by Frieda Lawrence; "The Piano," "Violets for
the Dead," "Glory of Darkness," "Violets," "Renascence," "Morality,"
and "Bavarian Gentians," copyright © 1964 by Angelo Ravagli and
C. Montague Weekley, Executors of The Estate of Frieda Lawrence
Ravagli, from *The Complete Poems of D. H. Lawrence*, 2 vols. (New
York: Viking Press, 1964), reprinted by permission of The Viking Press,
Inc.

Marianne Moore, "Poetry," *Collected Poems* (New York: Macmillan,
1963), copyright © 1935 by Marianne Moore, renewed 1963 by Marianne
Moore and T. S. Eliot, reprinted by permission of the publisher.

Wilfred Owen, "Anthem for Doomed Youth," "The Send-Off," "The
Last Laugh," "The Dead-Beat," "S. I. W.," "Inspection," "Soldier's
Dream," "To My Friend," "1914," and "Smile, Smile, Smile," copyright
© 1946, 1963 by Chatto & Windus, Ltd., from *Collected Poems*, edited
with an introduction and notes by C. Day Lewis and with a memoir
by Edmund Blunden (New York: New Directions, 1963), reprinted by
permission of New Directions Publishing Corp.

M. R. Ridley, *Keats' Craftsmanship: A Study in Poetic Development*
(Oxford: Clarendon Press, 1933; New York: Russell & Russell, 1962).

Dylan Thomas, "The Hunchback in the Park," "After the Funeral,"
"On the Marriage of a Virgin," "The tombstone told when she died,"
"And death shall have no dominion," "If I were tickled by the rub of
love," "Especially when the October wind," and "The force that through
the green fuse drives the flower," copyright © 1938, 1939, 1943, 1957
by New Directions Publishing Corp., from *Collected Poems* (New York:
New Directions, 1952), reprinted by permission of New Directions
Publishing Corp. "The minute is a prisoner in the hour" and drafts
of eight poems listed above, copyright © 1967 by The Trustees for the
Copyrights of Dylan Thomas, from Ralph Maud, ed., *The Notebooks
of Dylan Thomas* (New York: New Directions, 1967), reprinted by permission of New Directions Publishing Corp.

William Butler Yeats, "A Cradle Song," "The Sorrow of Love,"
"A Dream of Death," "The Hosting of the Sidhe," "The Two Trees,"
and "The Cap and Bells," copyright © 1906 by The Macmillan Company, renewed 1934 by W. B. Yeats; "Leda and the Swan," copyright ©
1928 by The Macmillan Company, renewed 1956 by Georgie Yeats;
"The Second Coming," copyright © 1924 by The Macmillan Company,
renewed 1952 by Bertha Georgie Yeats; "Byzantium," copyright © 1933
by The Macmillan Company, renewed 1961 by Bertha Georgie Yeats;
"The Circus Animals' Desertion," copyright © 1940 by Georgie Yeats,
renewed 1968 by Bertha Georgie Yeats, Michael Butler Yeats and Anne
Yeats, from Peter Allt and Russell K. Alspach, eds., *The Variorum Edition of the Poems of W. B. Yeats* (New York: Macmillan, 1957), reprinted by permission of The Macmillan Company, Michael B. Yeats
and The Macmillan Company of Canada.

TO

M. L. Rosenthal,

poet and teacher to poets

Preface

Visions and Revisions is a textual, direct approach to poetry. Each poem included in the book is preceded by at least one earlier draft or version of that poem. Such a format will allow us to explore the poet's vision from several perspectives. The commentary and questions following each poem intend to pull the reader into the poem, where he will be able to perceive not only the language of poetry, but the intrinsic values of language itself. This book should serve all students of poetry whether or not in an academic setting.

The poets represented were chosen primarily because of the availability of the materials needed for this study, the first drafts and revisions of their poems. The selection of poetry in each chapter is not necessarily representative of the individual poet's life work. The poems were chosen, rather, because of the insights offered by their various versions. In each instance, the A version is the final version. Earlier drafts are labeled B, C, and so on, depending on their number. However, because many of the poems underwent an even more extensive process of reworking, variant words or lines are also presented within these drafts. These further variants or deletions are indicated by brackets.

For the most part, the poets are chronologically arranged so that the sensitive reader may notice an historical development in the use of language, idiom, cadence, and tone. The exceptions are the Keats chapter, because it deals with only one long poem and is therefore more difficult in terms of this book's technique of examination, and the Blake chapter, because it presents a unique dimension for study. In a strictly chronological positioning, though, Blake would be first. All the other chapters contain a number of poems by a single poet, while the final chapter offers a miscellany of poets and their poems. In addition, there is an appendix of translated poems that illustrates how one vision—the original poem—can, when filtered through the medium of another language and seen through another man's eyes, give rise to a very different poem because of the translator's unique perception and use of language. A glossary of poetic terms has been included that provides brief definitions of those terms most commonly used in the discussion and analysis of poetry. The student will find many of these terms used and defined within the commentaries as well. In the glossary, examples have been drawn, where possible, from the poems in the book.

To avoid repetition in the commentary and the suggested questions, there is, so far as these are concerned, a progression from chapter to chapter. For example, the Emily Dickinson chapter illustrates extensive editorial changes involving syntax and punctuation. While the questions asked regarding the Dickinson material should serve as a further guide throughout the book, they are not repeated chapter to chapter. This is not to suggest, however, that the poetry progresses from easy to difficult.

In other words, the reader's approach must be a cumulative one, the observations gathered from one chapter enlarging the perspective for the ones to follow. Some questions may overlap, but others will drop off, and the reader may add his own. Additional points collect as the method accustoms one to question generally and achieve an expansive reading. The commentary also includes remarks that have no questions attached. These merely offer additional information or perhaps the author's point of view, and are intended as helpful guides to further questions.

There should be consistent inquiry about each poem, that is, which poem do I like best of the two or three versions and why? The commentary avoids repeating this question, but the exercise of looking at the revisions from this point of view is a valuable one. The serious questioning as to why a particular art object is favored over another ought eventually to lead away from the reader's own prejudices and toward that object under attention.

There were many people who helped in making this book. First of all, I extend my gratitude to Professor Leo Hamalian of the City College of New York who encouraged me to develop what was at first an idea and a classroom exercise into a book-length study. Also I thank Professors Paul Oppenheimer and Robert Ghiradella of CCNY and John Tytell of Queens College for their very careful and close reading of much of the material. I am indebted to Stephen and Elaine Aronoff for their special kindness and valuable suggestions. I am grateful to Eileen Penn, who typed the manuscript and provided editorial assistance. Also I thank my editor, Lloyd Scott, who encouraged this project, and Linda Lumley of the Crowell College Department, who was extremely helpful with the manuscript in its final stages.

B. W.

Contents

Introduction

. . . man can make statements about
verifiable facts: that is science. He
can develop extremely complex attitudes of self-adjustment towards
those facts: that is poetry.

STEPHEN SPENDER

I

Visions and Revisions presents various sets of poems,
each set containing two or more versions or stages of the
same poem. Frequently, one version will differ enough from
the other to communicate a slightly different, or even a vastly
different, experience. The quality of this altered experience
may not be easy to perceive, but the reader, whether or not
he can enunciate his perceptions, will feel the change.

The process of revision is basically an author working his
initial perception or vision through a first pattern (the first
version), then a second pattern, and so forth. Since the poet
is always organizing the various components of his response,
the versions represent a kind of jockeying for position as the
poet's attitude toward his initial experience or idea shifts. A
minor change in rhythm, image, or tone will often indicate
such shifting of attitude or reorganizing of response. Actually,
we see the poet's perception or vision become reset as the
language and music of the poetry changes. The poem may
contain a single idea or the retelling of an old story which
in each version remains fundamentally unchanged, while
oddly enough the experience itself changes each time the
words change. It is not necessarily the idea on which the

poem rests, nor the story it tells, that determines the poem's essence, but rather the language. A poem is determined by how the poet presents his own experience, imagined or real, with vital language and the sense of integrity that the relationship between language and experience suggests. Of course, other values condition a poem's life as well. Its life gains from and is informed by the reader's life.

In coming close to a poem through a number of its forms, we can break away from the false and distracting assumption that the key to the poem is "the idea the poet is trying to get across," or the story he is trying to relate. We will observe many examples where the general idea and plot remain fixed throughout the versions, yet their gestating visions offer the reader two very separate experiences, as different as unrelated poems.

Poems are often presented as pieces in a museum are—cold, perfect, and distant objects. There is little sense of the aesthetic process, or for that matter, the aesthetic reality of a poem, because the student's first contact with the poem is with a finished and apparently inspired work. The popular conception of the poet as madman or simply inspired artist needs to be dispelled, or when the truth is such, needs to be illuminated by closer contact with the poetic process. Another reaction is unquestioning respect, or even dismissal as irrelevant, of the poetry of great and famous authors. The approach of traditional anthologies encourages awe, which often fosters incomprehension and distrust, which in turn foster boredom.

Through the examination of poetic composition, the separation of the reader from the poem is diminished. As the reader moves closer to the poem, he moves closer to the artistic experience. The activity of seeing a poem closely includes a study of those techniques that control and create the poem, using illustrations from the various versions of the poem. Specifically, it is possible to observe how sound changes through the revision of merely a word or syllable, or through the shifting of a stress. Also, we may notice the effectiveness of different figures of speech, as, for example, when the extension of a metaphor throughout a stanza intensifies the language while leaving the prose meaning alone. Thus, the reader is able to see the poet as a builder, mechanic, and craftsman, as well as a thinker, "feeler," and creator.

Another barrier to the discovery of poetry is the require-ment of a prose paraphrase to understand the poem. The dif-ferent versions of the poem will absorb many questions con-cerned with matters of literal or intellectual meaning, what in some approaches is called prose meaning. Earlier versions may more explicitly express a point of view, tone, or story, and a combination of versions can make more apparent the direction of the poet's intentions.

Poetry demands a concentration that can accept a language of ideas and emotion that cannot be translated. A translation of experience, ideas, and emotions into handier forms or ex-pressions keeps us from both poetry and experience. A love affair examined in terms of needs and desires does not de-scribe what the participants feel, nor their experience. Poetry is difficult when we allow conventionality to bully us, to assign formulas, rules, or slogans to experience. Poetry, being so specific, cannot be translated. It must be left alone, so that the poem's meaning or meanings remain suggestive as well as true.

The questions about a poet, that is, what kinds of statements he makes, what he believes in, where he stands philosophi-cally, whether he is an optimist or pessimist, and so forth, however interesting they may be incidentally, rarely lead the student to the actuality of the poem. A comparison of early workshop drafts to the final version shows that philosophy, ideas, and opinions do not define or establish the poet or the art.

What the poem's philosophical position or motivating idea is can be a guide for the presentation of a reality that holds up a strange mirror to the original conception, fracturing it into several possible developments. The final poem, especially one that is the culmination of many manuscript drafts, may capture a more complex and also more exact truth than the original version. An exact poetic utterance, a demonstrable truth when we apply those standards found in the world of the poem itself, is realized when the weight of systematic reasoning has been eliminated as it is when we study the

poet's work on his developing personal vision. The beauty
that results from clear, logical thought is still present, but
the evidence of the ponderous labor necessary for its achievement has been removed.

This book is an inquiry into poetic pleasure. At the center
of the pleasure is the poem's elusiveness and, at the same
time, its simplicity. This simplicity is often overlooked because we have generally felt that great poetry ought to contain noble, broad, and powerful statements about the condition
of human affairs. Those questions, "What is the poet saying?"
or "What is the message of the poem?" are often masks for
"Which popular or unpopular platitude can I ascribe to this
or that poem?" The kind of truth a poet reveals is most difficult to paraphrase, not because of its profundity or obscurity, but because it is particular to the poet and to a very
short space of experience in the poet's life. It is this uniqueness that may anticipate the large questions of human nature.

When I. A. Richards wrote, ". . . good poetry owes its
value in a large measure to the closeness of its contact with
reality, it may thereby become a powerful weapon for breaking up unreal ideas and responses," he was speaking of a
relationship with reality that is encouraged by the poet's accommodating several feelings, responses, ideas, and levels of
experience at the same time. As the poet's vision may be informed by opposing positions and sympathies, he must also
be able to express the often paradoxical nature of his relationship to experience. The poet's ability to include such
variety and reality in his vision produces poetry's elusiveness,
its freedom from artificiality, that is, its simplicity. The poet's
desire to order this complex of attitudes and responses into a
recognizable design of certain clarity and concision produces
poetry's beauty.

II

Intimacy with the poem itself is the primary reason for this
book, and all the discussions are directed to achieving this
end. The method used is the study of language in a highly
focused manner. Additional insight into the creative process

will follow. This recognition of the processes of composition or the creative process will always be an incomplete one and, for some, a frustrating one.

Our imagination, as it is exposed in many ways to the poet's craftsmanship, may construct a creative process. When an image in an earlier draft is replaced by a different one in a later draft, we can imagine why the poet chose to do such a thing. Our imagining in this way is a particular method of paying attention to an artist as he exercises discrimination and develops his finished work. While never fully identifying the mental or internal activity of the poet, the conjectures about such activity are fascinating.

What is discovered is the development of poetic objectivity. In the revision of earlier and more autobiographical drafts, the development of an antiself or objective expression of the poet's own self is revealed. It is helpful to observe what the poet works away from, what he avoids. When the poet deletes certain passages or strikes out single words or shifts pauses, he is not only demonstrating his mastery over the craft, but at times showing his impatience or dissatisfaction with a part of himself when he was younger, even if the vision under the knife of correction is only five minutes old.

To go slightly further, each poem a poet writes is in some way a version of an earlier one, and in the same sense, all his poems are an attempt to write the poem that will best record himself and his experience. Through the versions of single poems and through groups of finished poems we see the poet charting his life and eventually the life and conditions of his age and city.

Just as poems are records of the experience of individuals in their times, the changes a poet makes over a period of time will in many cases expose more than his increasing technical efficiency as a craftsman and self-critic. The changes will record how and in what ways language is alive and in flux, reflecting many facets of our shifting mores, customs, and attitudes. The use of language is a gauge of how we live in the world. It, perhaps more than any other human institution, exposes the evolution of a society, not so much in the definitions of words, but in the implied communications. Yeats used an expression, "full round moon," in 1893, though by the time he collected his poems in 1933, the phrase was eliminated. Possibly Yeats decided it was a cliché or no longer romantically effective. Perhaps the change may indicate a shift in the way we look at the celestial bodies. Our entire system of faith may be at the center of the poet's decision. One generation may feel a certain way toward an event, story, or condition, and the next will either topple or intensify the received attitudes.

W. H. Auden's poetry offers another illustration. During the 1930's, the poet was involved in left-wing politics, an involvement reflecting an entire generation's hopes, aspirations, and frustrations. By the early 1950's Auden deleted lines and stanzas, and even whole poems from his *Collected Poetry*, indicating his, and a generation's, political disillusionment. The way a poet handles his language and his work over a period of time not only has poetical and historical significance, but becomes part of the study of mankind.

The values and the tensions of a particular era reveal themselves to the analytical eye of a literary historian. This fruitful activity may be matched by the critic of poetry. A close reading of contemporary poetry intensifies one's understanding of patterns of order, or chaos, in the contemporary world. The order poets perceive and construct out of the chaos and fertility of their own imaginations is the very order applied by "scientist, statesman, professional classes and eventually tradesmen," to use Stephen Spender's listing. The poets see this order first, in the same way poets are the first to detect, or at least expose, national disorder, and they discover rhythms in language to imitate such disorder. The imitation of life in art need not be construed as disorderly poetry imitating the disorder in the world or complex poetry following the recognition of complexity. Rather, it is a reciprocal relationship, revealing the basic ground of reality in the poet's achievement.

For reasons suggested above, contemporary poetry is often unpopular. After all, if the sounds and patterns of ideas, and evolving order or disorder, are not yet manifest to the general reader, he is likely to resist these patterns in the poetry he reads. The reader must be a participant in a world entirely new to him. This new world, an artificial construct, is the poem. He may perceive that this poem is an image of his actual world earlier unperceived by him. This intensified perception into one or another pattern comprises aesthetic pleasure, a reaction that still remains the most important reason for looking at art, or anything else for that matter.

To get close to poetry as experience, poetry as a particular kind of knowledge of the real world, we are looking here at revisions. There is an underlying consideration to bear in mind regarding all measurement or evaluation of the revisions. Since our attention will be directed to technical details, the illusion may be created that through these details alone we can understand why or how a poem moves or affects us. Just as the poet has no set rules he can apply, for he often succeeds in the most outrageous and unexpected ways, the reader must not expect to learn a right way to respond to a poem or analyze how it is affective.

Some poets create finished works without going through an extremely laborious process of revision. Some do work through copious drafts, others even work from prose sheets. Often the final draft, while far superior to the first version, differs only in a few details. Many poets produce a final version that has moved so far from the first draft as hardly to resemble it.

If the poet's vision is a true one, in the sense of seeing into the essential as well as the substantial level of experience, the vision will evoke in the reader a response something like a "moment of recognition." This powerful recognition is not of what the reader has already experienced, but of what he is experiencing at the moment of reading the poem. The reader of a Shakespearean sonnet denies himself a higher pleasure if he believes that he is enjoying the experience of reading the poem because he has already felt that experience, or a similar experience. Shakespeare's experience, however mundane or however noble, was unique, and the reader, however worldly, has never felt it. Once the poem, with *its* experience, is revealed to the reader, then he can have the poem's unique experience forever. The finest poetry is new life experience.

Some reader may ask, "If the poet's vision is such a power-ful one, then why all these stumblings to express what he is trying to say?" One answer is that while the matter or theme may not be overly complicated—about a man stopping by woods, or a man in love—the poet has the double task of envisioning and communicating his felt experience, while transforming language into art. So that this experience may be opened to the audience, the poet must labor to reproduce it in such a fashion that it remain his experience while not being private, and that it be public without being obvious. Poetry ought never be obvious in the sense that it would be predictable and standard. The poet must provide surprises to our senses and enrich our entire sensibility.

The most familiar poem will, if it is a good one, continue to surprise us and continue to be new. This is a mysterious and beautiful phenomenon in art, not entirely fathomed by our psychological sophistication. For this reason, the so-called "right reading" of a poem is often difficult to obtain. Some poems have about as many readings as there are critics. The poem may not be particularly obscure, but as with every new thing, we must reassess our own values when contacting it. Literary criticism is, in part, the activity of rebuilding and redefining values and attitudes toward experience often very foreign to us. While many critics will agree on the poem's basic meaning, tone, and structure, there may be facets of the poem's being that remain wonderfully elusive. For literary criticism, as for the study of the creative process, the clues that emerge in the earlier drafts are illuminating. However, this ought not be overemphasized. Early versions are richer, more valuable than when used merely as tables to compre-hend a complex experience which is the final draft. Each poem stands on its own, impenetrable from the outside. You must finally get inside in order to read it.

We often take it for granted that the poet who is master of his craft will produce in his final version his best poem. We assume that though the poet may sacrifice many lovely touches and lines, he will finally make his poem better in the final analysis. If the reader follows this assumption too religiously, he will miss the point that the two versions often present not merely a poem getting better, but two separate experiences, each valuable and interesting in its own right. Too, it is possible for the poet, with his eye and sensibility controlled by many concerns, to make his final poem best in relation to his developing vision, but inferior to the earlier version. Again, I am asking for fresh attention not only to every poet and every final poem, but to each and every version and revision.

> A Poem . . . is in every sense a teaching machine for the training of perception and judgment.
>
> MARSHALL MC LUHAN

> Criticism, as I understand it, is the endeavor to discriminate between experiences and evaluate them.
>
> I. A. RICHARDS

III

There is a final question: Why bother with these poems at all? or more explicitly: What is the ultimate value of poetry and criticism after all? Or as I. A. Richards asks the question, "Why are . . . [poems] worth the devotion of the keenest hours of the best minds, what is their place in this system of human endeavors?" If our concern is to be with poetic value, poetic pleasure, we must have a good, strong conviction about poetry's values.

Clearly the poet who writes

Ah, love, let us be true
To one another! for the world, which seems
To lie before us like a land of dreams,
So various, so beautiful, so new,
Hath really neither joy, nor love, nor light,
Nor certitude, nor peace, nor help for pain;
And we are here as on a darkling plain
Swept with confused alarms of struggle and flight,
Where ignorant armies clash by night.

is doing something very different from making a statement such as "Certain difficult periods in history produce a desperate need for love." His verses may imply such a statement, but poetry magnifies the specific recollection of experience and this statement, like most prose statements, is a generalization that could include a great variety of possible human experiences.

The states of mind poetry generates, how the activity of the poem affects us, is apparently a far different consideration from how the poem evolves into its form of art. That last consideration involves poetry's technical qualities. However, since it is through these techniques that the poem is formed, we must pay close attention to the details, version to version, as our states of mind are being affected. The investigation of the particular features of the poem is criticism. Through the critical method of making discriminations regarding various objects, in this case, poems, and by noting our responses to the poems' components, we approach an awareness of why and how different things affect us. With our responses to the special features of a poem, changing techniques in some cases, lie the clues to how we feel first about the poem, next about our own lives in relation to the poem, and ultimately about the world.

Even the barest poetry works through images. Words that can devise something new out of their own being, cause imagined uniqueness, are like wonderful tools used in the making of a new thing. While the poet is "making it new" in this way, he is, at the same time, consciously or unconsciously storing, preserving, and possibly transcending the values of his own age. The extent to which the poet is involved with these values often determines his image-making facilities. Reading poetry not only extends our world through images, but delivers and connects us to various systems of values. In learning to make a most intimate contact with value systems we may be better able to make free choices. For once we are able to evaluate another's vision, perception, or system of beliefs, it will be less likely that any system of values will be forced on us, for we will be able to discriminate.

Emily Dickinson

1830—1886

Tell all the Truth but tell it slant—
Success in Circuit lies
Too bright for our infirm Delight
The Truths superb surprise.

As Lightning to the Children eased
With explanation kind
The Truth must dazzle gradually
Or every man be blind—

Wᴇ have Thomas H. Johnson to thank for his excellent variorum edition of *The Poems of Emily Dickinson* (Cambridge, 1955), which finally enabled readers of Emily Dickinson to study her poems as she had written them down. In the various editions that followed her death in 1886, editors altered and "regularized" the poems to suit the demands of popular taste. Only twelve poems were published in her lifetime.

Emily Dickinson lived her entire life in Amherst, Massachusetts, a village of stern Puritan origins, making only brief visits to South Hadley and Washington, D.C. Her father, a lawyer and congressman, was a friend of Ralph Waldo Emerson, and it is quite possible that as a young girl Emily may have met and listened to this leading American thinker and poet. It is necessary to remind ourselves that Emily Dickinson was involved in the literary and cultural world of her day. Because her life eventually became relatively reclusive, the tendency is to imagine it, inaccurately, as "a buried life." Emily Dickinson reached out to many people, largely through correspondence, and many of these people were aware of her poems. It is evident through her letters that she knew her poetic strength, which is attested to by her central question to her literary friend T. W. Higginson. She wanted to know if her verse was "alive," did it "breathe."

In his introduction, Johnson provides us with the reliable text of Dickinson's poems, and details the various editorial problems encountered in working with the manuscripts and various editions:

> The manuscripts of nearly all the poems survive. The text is always in one of three stages of composition: a fair copy, a semi-final draft, or a workshop draft. It sometimes had been set down in two or more various fair copies, sent to different friends. On occasion it is found in all three stages, thus affording the chance to watch the creative spirit in action.

Johnson makes it clear that one version is as valid, or as final, as another. The so-called authoritative version is often arbitrarily chosen. Occasionally there is evidence that the original inspiration produced a poem complete in its first draft, and that the poet was completely satisfied with it, for example, the famous "Humming Bird." But generally, there is no such indication as to which version the poet preferred, or if she was ever completely satisfied with the last version.

The external and, perhaps more important, internal events of Emily Dickinson's life are charted in her poems. Her many losses, her daily involvement with her natural surroundings, her growing and acute sensitivity to relationships—all are there. Yet an overemphasis on the autobiographical nature of her poetry tends to make one less aware of the revelation of a psychological dilemma that is truly universal in nature, a dilemma exemplified by her love of paradox—a bitter perception of contraries within single experiences. Both the short, epigrammatic line and the strange punctuation—her use of the dash—communicate a world in which reliance and faith are being constantly disturbed.

Her poems can be divided into general themes. Many of her love poems are about renunciation while others, though it is not often revealed in the typical anthology selections, are much more sensual. In the nature poems, one feels her

sensibility reaching out for truth through the creation of relationships with all things beyond the self, that is, with the
eternal. This extension to include the infinite contained in
spirit, nature, and man is part of her concept of "circumference":

Circumference, Thou Bride of Awe
Possessing thou shalt be,
Possessed by every hallowed knight
That dares to covet thee.

Her intent was to elicit awe, not dread (though fear is a dominant emotion in her poetry), and to send this awe out through
circumference. We can find analogies to her sense of awe in
the most religious poetry, yet her own sense is particularly
secular and metaphysical. Still, she is also moved by a sense
of the Creator. Awe in this sense also finds constant expression in her poetry.

There is also a grouping of poems having to do with
psychological pain, another with death. These divisions are
only convenient ways to categorize many overlapping themes.
Many of her poems are invested with them all.

Emily Dickinson is a nineteenth-century poet with many
of the characteristics typical of the late Romantic and Victorian ages. Stylistically, there is an obvious debt to Emerson
and to the seventeenth-century poet Sir Thomas Browne, but
more so to the Bible in her use of Biblical cadence and rhythm.
It has been said of her that "the Bible was her lexicon." Yet
modern critics and readers have embraced her poetry as if
it were modern. Cries of priggishness or lady-like poetry can
hardly apply, and her poems can undergo the careful examination that one would afford John Donne or T. S. Eliot. Her
imagery is both suggestive and vivid and invites the reader to
participate in the experience of the poem in a way that only
the most well-wrought poetry does.

The chronological arrangement here, as in Johnson's variorum edition, is merely an approximation. I have followed his
direction rather than that provided by *The Editing of Emily
Dickinson, a Reconsideration* by Ralph William Franklin, a
recent book which raises interesting questions about the

editing of the poems. The A version, in general, is the definitive poem as Johnson chooses to present it, though it is not
necessarily the final version the poet wrote. Likewise, in this
chapter only, B and C versions are not indicators of chronological order, but merely of the poet's variant version. Poems
marked X contain alterations made by one or another of Emily
Dickinson's editors. When relevant, notes, sources, and dates
of publication will be given following the poem.

A

Heart! We will forget him!
You and I—tonight!
You may forget the warmth he gave—
I will forget the light!

When you have done, pray tell me   5
That I may straight begin!
Haste! lest while you're lagging
I remember him!

X

Heart! We will forget him!
You and I tonight!
You may forget the warmth he gave
I will forget the light!

When you have done, pray tell me   5
That I my thoughts may dim
Haste! lest while you're lagging
I may remember him!

1. Emily Dickinson's use of dashes and other punctuation
is often idiosyncratic. When the editors regularized the punctuation here, did they make an easier flowing poem? In the

forthcoming poetry one might consider when her poetry invites editorial interference by its unconventionality. What else, other than tempo, is disturbed by the elimination of dashes? Why retain all exclamation points?

2. Why did the editors tamper with line 6? Is its tone at variance with the rest of the poem? Does it change the meaning?

3. Elements of emotional conflict are as essential to dramatic poetry as are the multiple voices and characters in a play. Multiple voices and characters, however, may be implied if not actually present. Discuss this poem as a drama. Such a discussion must consider tone of voice of one or another dramatic parts. In order for dramatic tension to be upheld, the dramatic voice must be consistent.

B

If those I loved were lost the criers
voice would tell me—
ne'er? [would.]
If those I loved were found the bells of
Ghent would ring.   5
Did those I love repose, The
Daisy would impel me—Philip
[questioned eager]
[I, my riddles bring] when bewildered
bore his riddle in—

A

If those I loved were lost
The Crier's voice w'd tell me—
If those I loved were found
The bells of Ghent w'd ring—
Did those I loved repose   5

The Daisy would impel me.
Philip—when bewildered
Bore his riddle in!

In *Bolts of Melody*, ed. Mabel Loomis Todd and Millicent
Todd Bingham (New York: Harper and Row, 1945), the
poem is arranged in two quatrains.

1. The odd syntax, or sentence structure, is retained from
the workshop draft to the final poem, yet the final poem is
very different. Does the visual set-up of the poem affect our
sense of it? For instance, what is the effect of making the
lines approximately the same length? How do visual techniques influence the way the poem sounds to us?

2. The poet will often abbreviate words for various pur-
poses. We must not consider an abbreviation, as in A2, a loss
of a beat or measure. After all, our minds still pronounce
"w'd" as would. Space *is* contained, however, creating the
illusion of a swifter moving line and rhythm may be thus
affected.

3. Does the deleted material in B provide clues to a reading
of the riddle? How much of the poem is a riddle anyway?

✻

B

Called Back

Just lost, when I was saved!
Just heard the world go by!
Just girt me for the onset with Eternity
When breath drew back,
And on the other side   5
I heard recede the disappointed tide!

Therefore, as One returned, I feel,
Odd secrets of "the Line" to tell!

Some Sailor, skirting novel shores
Some pale "reporter" from the awful doors   10
Before the Seal!

Next time, to stay!
Next time, the things to see
By Ear unheard,
Unscrutinized by Eye —   15
Next time, to tarry,
While the Ages steal —
Tramp the slow centuries, ✗
And the Cycles wheel!

A

Just lost, when I was saved!
Just felt the world go by!
Just girt me for the onset with Eternity,
When breath blew back,
And on the other side   5
I hear recede the disappointed tide!

Therefore, as One returned, I feel,
Odd secrets of the line to tell!
Some Sailor, skirting foreign shores—
Some pale Reporter, from the awful doors   10
Before the Seal!

Next time, to stay!
Next time, the things to see
By Ear unheard,
Unscrutinized by Eye—   15

Next time, to tarry,
While the Ages steal—
Slow tramp the Centuries, ✗
And the Cycles wheel!

1. "Novel shores" in B9, while carrying the same literal meaning as "foreign shores" in A9, is a very different construction. The phrase used in A is less strange. After all, we understand "novel" only in terms of the shores' being foreign (new to sailors) in the first place. Because the one is more metaphysical, less direct, than the other does not mean it produces better poetry. Certain metaphors offer false attractiveness.

2. Line 18 is different in each version. How different is the meaning of each? Consider whether or not this is a significant change. Discuss the question of consistency of diction or language usage in the poem regarding this change in line 18.

3. What is implied about the author's attitude toward the words in quotation marks?

B

I taste a liquor never brewed—
From Tankards scooped in Pearl—
Not all the Frankfort Berries
Yield such an Alcohol!

Inebriate of Air—am I—   5
And Debauchee of Dew—
Reeling—thro endless summer days—
From inns of Molten Blue—

When "Landlords" turn the drunken Bee
Out of the Foxglove's door—   10
When Butterflies—renounce their "drams"—
I shall but drink the more!

Till Seraphs swing their snowy Hats—
And Saints—to windows run—
To see the little Tippler   15
From Manzanilla come!

𝒜

I taste a liquor never brewed—
From Tankards scooped in Pearl—
Not all the Vats upon the Rhine
Yield such an Alcohol!

Inebriate of Air—am I—   5
And Debauchee of Dew—
Reeling—thro endless summer days—
From inns of Molten Blue—

When "Landlords" turn the drunken Bee
Out of the Foxglove's door—   10
When Butterflies—renounce their "drams"—
I shall but drink the more!

Till Seraphs swing their snowy Hats—
And Saints—to windows run—
To see the little Tippler   15
Leaning against the—Sun—

*In an edition published after her death, editors altered the
first stanza to read:*

I taste a liquor never brewed,
From tankards scooped in pearl;
Not Frankfort berries yield the sense
Such a delirious whirl.

1. The editors in 1861 felt the need to alter line B4. Is the
original line objectionable? What conjectures can be made
about editorial taste during this period?

2. "Manzanilla" in B16 *is* a better sounding word in the
context of line 15. The line is more melodious than A16.
However, while A16 may seem more prosaic, the language
being direct, it does achieve a necessary image. It is a difficult
image to conceive of but in the context of the whole last
stanza, it does make sense. After all, the Saints are doing
the seeing here. Is there something about the second stanza

or the general mood of the entire poem that accounts for the last line in A?

3. Is the rhythm improved or disturbed by the alteration of line 3? Which line holds richer imagery? Specificity is lost when "Frankfort Berries" is abandoned. What is gained?

C

Safe in their Alabaster Chambers—
Untouched by Morning
And untouched by Noon—
Sleep the meek members of the Resurrection—
Rafter of satin,   5
And Roof of stone.

Light laughs the breeze
In her Castle above them—
Babbles the Bee in a stolid Ear,
Pipe the Sweet Birds in ignorant cadence—   10
Ah, what sagacity perished here!

B

Safe in their Alabaster Chambers—
Untouched by Morning—
And untouched by Noon—
Sleep the meek members of the Resurrection,
Rafter of Satin—and Roof of Stone—   5

Grand go the Years,
In the Crescent above them—
Worlds scoop their Arcs—
And Firmaments—row—
Diadems—drop—   10

And Doges—surrender—
Soundless as Dots,
On a Disc of Snow.

A

Safe in their Alabaster Chambers,
Untouched by Morning—
And Untouched by Noon—
Lie the meek members of the Resurrection—
Rafter of Satin—and Roof of Stone—   5

Grand go the Years—in the Crescent—above them—
Worlds scoop their Arcs—
And Firmaments—row—
Diadems—drop—and Doges—surrender
Soundless as dots—on a Disc of Snow—   10

> This poem was enclosed in a letter to Sue Dickinson in
> 1861.

Substitute stanzas for second stanza sent to Sue:

Springs—shake the sills—
But—the Echoes—stiffen—
Hoar—is the window—
And numb the door—
Tribes of Eclipse—in Tents—of Marble—   5
Staples—of Ages—have buckled—there—

Springs—shake the Seals—
But the silence—stiffens—
Frosts unhook—in the Northern Zones—
Icicles—crawl from the Polar Caverns—
Midnight in Marble—Refutes—the Suns—   5

X

Safe in their Alabaster Chambers—
Untouched by Morning
And untouched by Noon—
Sleep the meek members of the Resurrection—
Rafter of satin, And Roof of Stone.   5

Light laughs the breeze
In her Castle of sunshine
Babbles the Bee in a stolid Ear.
Pipe the Sweet Birds in ignorant cadence—
Ah, what sagacity perished here!   10

Grand go the Years—in the Crescent—above them—
Worlds scoop their Arcs—
And Firmaments—row—
Diadems—drop—and Doges surrender
Soundless as dots—on a Disc of Snow—   15

1. The lyric is a short poem, usually on a theme of personal love or sorrow. It is marked by its personal tone as well as its apparent spontaneity. It is like a short burst of song, sudden, and "lyrical." In the above versions we see many changes, changes that actually embody different kinds of poetry. Where is Emily Dickinson practicing lyrical poetry with the particular intensity of that mode? When is she less lyrical, more intellectual? What kind of poem is finally achieved?

2. Which attempt at the second stanza is more musical? Consider all versions of the stanza. How is this an important consideration in this particular poem?

3. In her attempts to embody a vision that must have been shifting, she writes with entirely different images, movement, and ideas. The reconstructed version X is most interesting for it brings together two versions of the second stanza as its second and third stanzas. Do you think this is successful or is it an awkward construction?

4. "Castle of sunshine" in X7 sounds like a cliché and not very much like an Emily Dickinson metaphor. Can you characterize her metaphors?

B

He put the Belt around my life
I heard the Buckle snap—
And left his process satisfied
My Lifetime folding up—
Deliberate, as a Duke would do   5
A Kingdom's Title Deed—
Henceforth, a Dedicated sort—
A Member of the Cloud.

Yet near enough to come at call—
And do the little Toils   10
That make the Circuit of the Rest—
And deal occasional smiles
To lives as stoop to notice mine—
And kindly ask it in—
Whose invitation, For this world   15
For Whom I must decline?

            Incorporating suggested variants.

A

He put the Belt around my life
I heard the Buckle snap—
And turned away, imperial,
My Lifetime folding up—
Deliberate as a Duke would do   5
A Kingdom's Title Deed—
Henceforth, a Dedicated sort—
A Member of the Cloud.

Yet not too far to come at call—
And do the little Toils   10
That make the Circuit of the Rest—
And deal the occasional smiles
To lives that stoop to notice mine—
And kindly ask it in—
Whose invitation, know you not   15
For Whom I must decline?

> In *Poems* (1891), one word is altered: l. 15: know/knew.

1. The two versions are from one manuscript poem. The B version includes the poet's canceled or marginal lines and words. What results from this editorial process is two versions of the same poem, when in fact there were not two versions intended but rather one poem with certain undecided parts.

2. In B3 "process" is an interesting word when referring to an act of love or human contact—both of which are implied in the first two lines. Yet the word "process" is extremely cold. There may be a built-in slur in her usage. The line, however, is difficult to read aloud and in respect to euphony A3 sounds much better. Belt/life/Buckle/imperial form a lovely pattern of sounds. Is more lost than gained in line 3? Does "imperial" do more than merely sound good?

3. Note how the action and attention in A3 remain with the "He" of the first line. In the B version "He" is dismissed earlier.

4. What does the apparently minor change in line 9 indicate about the speaker's attitude toward her situation? Discuss the other changes.

B

I felt a Funeral, in my Brain,
And Mourners to and fro
Kept treading—treading—till it seemed
That Sense was breaking through—

And when they all were seated,   5
A Service, like a Drum—
Kept beating—beating—till I thought
My mind was going numb—

And then I heard them lift a Box
And creak across my Soul   10
With those same Boots of Lead, again,
Then Space—began to toll,

As all the Heavens were a Bell,
And Being, but an Ear,
And I, and Silence, some strange Race   15
Wrecked, and solitary, here—

And then a Plank in Reason, broke,
And I dropped down, and down—
And hit a World, at every Crash
And Got through—knowing then—   20

          Incorporating suggested variants.

A

I felt a Funeral, in my Brain,
And Mourners to and fro
Kept treading—treading—till it seemed
That Sense was breaking through—

And when they all were seated,   5
A Service, like a Drum—
Kept beating—beating—till I thought
My mind was going numb—

And then I heard them lift a Box
And creak across my Soul   10
With those same Boots of Lead, again,
Then Space—began to toll,

As all the Heavens were a Bell,
And Being, but an Ear,
And I, and Silence, some strange Race   15
Wrecked, and solitary, here—

And then a Plank in Reason, broke,
And I dropped down, and down—
And hit a World, at every plunge,
And Finished knowing—then—   20

> In *Poems* (1896), this poem was printed with stanza 5
> omitted.

1. This often-reprinted poem conveys psychological pain.
The pain felt in the first stanza is perceived in a context of
disorder and is later organized through images of the funeral
service and intensified in the terrifying stanza 3. From this
point, the poem moves toward the reception of stanza 5.
In 1896 the editors omitted this fifth stanza. Does stanza 4
seem to offer a solution as to why they did this "chopping"?
2. A different idea develops because of the few variants
in the last lines. The shift in tone suggests a psychological
difference as well.

B

There came a Day—at Summer's full—
Entirely for me—
I thought that such—were for the Saints—
Where Resurrections [Revelations]—be—

The Sun—as Common—went abroad   5
The Flowers accustomed blew
While our two Souls that [As if no Souls the] Solstice
          passed—
Which [that] maketh all things new.

The time was scarce profaned—by speech—
The falling [figure/symbol] of a word   10
Was needless—as at Sacrament—
The wardrobe—of our Lord—

Each was to each—the sealed church—
Permitted to commune—this time—
Lest we too awkward—show—   15
At "Supper of the Lamb."

The hours slid fast—as hours will—
Clutched tight—by greedy hands—
So—faces on two Decks—look back—
Bound to opposing lands—   20

And so—when all the time had leaked [failed]—
Without external sound—
Each—bound the other's Crucifix—
We gave no other bond—

Sufficient troth—that we shall rise—   25
Deposed—at length—the Grave—
To that New Marriage—
Justified—through Calvaries of Love!

A

There came a Day at Summer's full,
Entirely for me—
I thought that such were for the Saints,
Where Resurrections—be—

The Sun, as common, went abroad,   5
The flowers, accustomed, blew,
As if no soul the solstice passed
That maketh all things new—

The time was scarce profaned, by speech—
The symbol of a word   10
Was needless, as at Sacrament,
The Wardrobe—of our Lord—

Each was to each The Sealed Church,
Permitted to commune this—time—
Lest we too awkward show   15
At Supper of the Lamb.

The Hours slid fast—as Hours will,
Clutched tight, by greedy hands—
So faces on two Decks, look back,
Bound to opposing lands—   20

And so when all the time had leaked,
Without external sound
Each bound the Other's Crucifix—
We gave no other Bond—

Sufficient troth, that we shall rise—   25
Deposed—at length, the Grave—
To that new Marriage,
Justified—through Calvaries of Love—

> This poem was published in *Scribner's Magazine*, VIII
> (August, 1890), titled "Renunciation." Stanza 4 was
> omitted. The following words were altered: l. 3: were/
> was, l. 7: soul/sail, l. 17: fast/past, l. 25: shall/should.

1. The editor's alteration (see note below A) generally
makes the language more predictable, as if they suspect the
poet of being mad. For example, line 17: Slid "fast" is a

rather startling substitution for the more standard "slid past."
Yet it *does* much more, whatever problems the reader may
encounter.

2. Emily Dickinson's use of capital letters has caused much
wondering. How is the poet using capitalization as a device?

3. Discuss the intellectual struggle apparent in B10. Comment on the other variants bracketed in B.

4. Line 7 is different in meaning in the two versions. Here
the difference betrays the speaker's emotion rather than her
religious point of view.

5. Action and movement are finally sacrificed in A10. Is
"symbol" a better word?

A

I heard a Fly buzz—when I died—
The Stillness in the Room
Was like the Stillness in the Air—
Between the Heaves of Storm—

The Eyes around—had wrung them dry—   5
And Breaths were gathering firm
For that last Onset—when the King
Be witnessed—in the Room—

I willed my Keepsakes—Signed away
What portion of me be   10
Assignable—and then it was
There interposed a Fly—

With Blue—uncertain stumbling Buzz—
Between the light—and me—
And then the Windows failed—and then   15
I could not see to see—

X

Dying

I heard a Fly buzz—when I died—
The Stillness round my form
Was like the Stillness in the Air—
Between the Heaves of Storm—

The Eyes beside—had wrung them dry—   5
And Breaths were gathering sure
For that last Onset—when the King
Be witnessed—in his power—

I willed my Keepsakes—Signed Away
What portion of me—I   10
Could make assignable—and then
There interposed a Fly—

With Blue uncertain stumbling Buzz—
Between the light—and me—
And then the Windows failed—and then   15
I could not see to see—

1. In X2 "round" *is* more dramatic. Is the word preferred for this reason? How are other words, as in the second stanza, affected by the change?

2. What are the editors aiming at in the rewriting of line 8?

3. Note the editors' attempt to make lines 10 and 11 "easier." Both are difficult to read. Is this a weak point in the poem?

4. Comment on whatever specific changes affect the rhyming in this poem.

�

B

Dare you see a soul at the "White Heat?"
Then crouch within the door—
Red—is the Fire's common tint—
But when the quickened Ore

Has sated Flame's conditions—   5
She quivers from the Forge
Without a color, but the Light
Of unannointed Blaze—

Least Village, boasts its Blacksmith—
Whose Anvil's even ring   10
Stands symbol for the finer Forge
That soundless tugs—within—

Refining these impatient Ores
With Hammer, and with Blaze
Until the designated Light   15
Repudiate the Forge—

This version was published in the *Atlantic Monthly* (October, 1891) with Emily Dickinson's suggested variants: l. 4: quickened/vivid, l. 6: Its quivering substance plays, l. 10: ring/din.

In *Poems* (1891), the version of the poem is the same as that in the *Atlantic Monthly*, but it is titled "The White Heat."

A

Dare you see a Soul *at the White Heat?*
Then crouch within the door—
Red—is the Fire's common tint—
But when the vivid Ore
Has vanquished Flame's conditions,   5
It quivers from the Forge
Without a color, but the light

Of unannointed Blaze.
Least Village has its Blacksmith
Whose Anvil's even ring   10
Stands symbol for the finer Forge
That soundless tugs—within—
Refining these impatient Ores
With Hammer, and with Blaze
Until the Designated Light   15
Repudiate the Forge—

1. Does this poem naturally fall into stanzas or is the single
sixteen-line unit more consistent with the poem's design? If
both are acceptable but create different responses in the
reader, what is it about typography that does this?

2. Comment on the length and sound as well as the meanings of the two words changed in lines 4 and 5.

3. Why the change in pronoun in line 6? This may be a
matter of style, but the poet's choice could trigger a change
of attitude in the reader.

4. "Boasts" is a better word in line 9. But like a dominant
line in a painting, a word may pull too much attention
toward an action the poet does not want emphasized. Is this
the case here?

5. What is the dominant action or concern of the poem?
Is it the same—on all levels—in both versions?

A

Because I could not stop for Death—
He kindly stopped for me—
The Carriage held but just Ourselves—
And Immortality.

We slowly drove—He knew no haste   5
And I had put away
My labor and my leisure too,
For His Civility—

We passed the School, where Children strove
At Recess—in the Ring—   10
We passed the Fields of Grazing Grain—
We passed the Setting Sun—

Or rather—He passed Us—
The Dews drew quivering and chill—
For only Gossamer, my Gown—   15
My Tippet—only Tulle—

We paused before a House that seemed
A Swelling of the Ground—
The Roof was scarcely visible—
The Cornice—in the Ground—   20

Since then—'tis Centuries—and yet
Feels shorter than the Day
I first surmised the Horses Heads
Were toward Eternity—

X

The Chariot

Because I could not stop for Death—
He kindly stopped for me—
The Carriage held but just Ourselves—
And Immortality.

We slowly drove—He knew no haste   5
And I had put away
My labor and my leisure too,
For His Civility—

We passed the School, where Children played
Their lessons scarcely done.   10
We passed the Fields of Grazing Grain—
We passed the setting Sun—

We paused before a House that seemed
A Swelling of the Ground—
The Roof was scarcely visible—   15
The Cornice—but a Mound—

Since then—'tis Centuries—but each
Feels shorter than the Day
I first surmised the Horses Heads
Were toward Eternity—   20

1. For years critics of Emily Dickinson's poetry were dis-
tressed by the fact that her poetry had been mangled by editors. Mr. Johnson's text reveals qualities in many of the
poems which had been obscured by earlier editors. Note the
changes in lines 9 and 10. What has the poet—not the editors
—done to vary the rhythm of the line? How do the editors
create an image with one word in line 9 that the poet couldn't
possibly have intended?

2. There is an interesting play of the mind that is missed
by the editorial omission of stanza 4.

3. There are a few other changes in certain short words.
Do these count in terms of our responses?

B

My Life had stood—a Loaded Gun—
In Corners—till a Day—
The Owner passed—identified—
And carried Me away—

And now We roam the Sovreign Woods—   5
And now We hunt the Doe—
And every time I speak for Him—
The Mountains straight reply—

And do I smile, such cordial light
Upon the Valley glow—   10
It is as a Vesuvian face
Had let its pleasure through—

And when at Night—Our good Day done—
I guard my Master's Head—
'Tis better than the Eider-Duck's   15
Low Pillow—to have shared—

To foe of His—I'm deadly foe—
None harm the second time—
On whom I lay a Yellow Eye—
Or an emphatic Thumb—   20

Though I than He—may longer live
He longer must—than I—
For I have but the art to kill,
Without—the power to die—

Published in *London Mercury*, XIX (February, 1929);
variants in lines 5 and 23 were adopted for publication.

A

My Life had stood—a Loaded Gun—
In Corners—till a Day
The Owner passed—identified—
And carried Me away—

And now We roam in Sovreign Woods—   5
And now We hunt the Doe—
And every time I speak for Him—
The Mountains straight reply—

And do I smile, such cordial light
Upon the Valley glow—   10
It is as a Vesuvian face
Had let its pleasure through—

And when at Night—Our good Day done—
I guard my Master's Head—
'Tis better than the Eider-Duck's   15
Deep Pillow—to have shared—

To foe of His—I'm deadly foe—
None stir the second time—
On whom I lay a Yellow Eye—
Or an emphatic thumb—   20

Though I than He—may longer live
He longer must—than I—
For I have but the power to kill,
Without—the power to die—

1. The poet's aim is to embody experience through the use
of carefully selected and artful language. The techniques or
stylistic devices must not upstage that experience by calling
attention to themselves. On the other hand, artful contriv-
ances, special kinds of "lies," are often part of the poet's way
of telling special truths. The finest poetry achieves the exact
balance between telling direct truths and using artful devices.
Generally, the more complex the experience of the poem, the
more elaborate and numerous the devices used by the poet.

In light of the above, which version of line 5 is less artificial, and is it more or less successful?

2. How do the specific word changes in lines 16, 18, and 23
make the meaning of A clearer than B?

B

I felt a Cleaving in my Mind
As if my Brain had split
I tried to match it Seam by Seam
But could not make them fit.

The thought behind, I tried to join   5
Unto the thought before
But Sequence ravelled out of reach
Like Balls—upon a Floor.

Variant of second stanza:

The Dust behind I strove to join
Unto the Disk before—
But Sequence ravelled out of Sound
Like Balls upon a Floor—

A

I felt a Cleaving in my Mind—
As if my Brain had split—
I tried to match it Seam by Seam—
But could not make them fit.

The thought behind, I strove to join   5
Unto the thought before—
But Sequence ravelled out of Sound
Like Balls—upon a Floor.

> A version of this poem, titled "The Last Thought," was
> published in *Poems* (1896). The change in line 7 was
> adopted. Word altered: l. 1: Cleaving/cleavage.

1. The B version of the second stanza introduces an interesting conceit, or elaborated idea. Does this merely intensify
or build upon the already metaphysical imagery of the poem,
or is the pattern of imagery somehow changed?

2. Is "The Last Thought" an appropriate title? Are titles
important in poems?

3. Discuss the change of the first line in the version published in *Poems* (1896). Does the poem's "activity" demand a
participle? Would the noun be the more conservative choice?

4. Which version of line 7 is most consistent with the development of imagery in the poem?

B

Because that you are going
And never coming back
And I, however accurate [absolute],
May overlook [misinfer] your Track,
Because that Death is Treason [different],   5
However true [due] [just] [first] it be—
This instant be abolished [This instant be suspended]
To all but Fealty [Above Mortality]—

Significance [Omnipotence], that each has lived
The other to detect—   10
Discovery, not God himself
Could now annihilate.
Eternity, presumption,
The instant I perceive
That you who were existence   15
Yourself forgot to live—

"The life that is," will then have been
A thing I never knew,
As Paradise, fictitious,
Until the Realm of you.   20
The "Life that is to be" to me
A Residence too plain
Unless in my Redeemer's Face
I recognize your own—

Of Immortality who doubts   25
He may exchange [confer] with me
Curtailed by your obscuring [removing] Face
Of everything but he,

Of Heaven and Hell I also yield
The Right to reprehend   30
To whoso would commute this Face
For his less priceless Friend—

If "God is Love" as he admits,
We think that he must be
Because he is a jealous God   35
He tells us certainly.
If "All is possible" with him
As he besides concedes,
He will refund us finally
Our confiscated Gods—   40

A

Because that you are going
And never coming back
And, I however absolute
May overlook your Track—

Because that Death is final,   5
However first it be
This instant be suspended
Above Mortality—

Significance that each has lived
The other to detect   10
Discovery not God himself
Could now annihilate

Eternity, Presumption
The instant I perceive
That you, who were Existence   15
Yourself forgot to live—

The "Life that is" will then have been
A thing I never knew—

As Paradise fictitious
Until the Realm of you—   20

The "Life that is to be," to me,
A Residence too plain
Unless in my Redeemer's Face
I recognize your own—

Of Immortality who doubts   25
He may exchange with me
Curtailed by your obscuring Face
Of everything but He—

Of Heaven and Hell I also yield
The right to reprehend   30
To whoso would commute this Face
For his less priceless Friend.

If "God is Love" as he admits
We think that he must be
Because he is a "jealous God"   35
He tells us certainly

If "All is possible with" him
As he besides concedes
He will refund us finally
Our confiscated Gods—   40

1. Does the B version, with its various choices of words, suggest additional clues to the poem's meaning? There is no doubt that the poem must finally communicate entirely on its own, but a view into the poetic process is often illuminating by freshly directing attention to specific words and phrases.

B

To pity those who [that] know her not
Is helped [soothed] by the regret
That those who know her know her less
The nearer her they get—
How adequate the Human Heart   5
To its emergency
Intrenchments stimulate [Intrenchment stimulates] a friend
And stem [stems] [balk] an enemy

A

What mystery pervades a well!
The water lives so far—
A neighbor from another world
Residing in a jar

Whose limit none have ever seen,   5
But just his lid of glass—
Like looking every time you please
In an abyss's face!

The grass does not appear afraid,
I often wonder he   10
Can stand so close and look so bold
At what is awe to me.

Related somehow they may be,
The sedge stands next the sea—
Where he is floorless   15
And does not timidity betray

But nature is a stranger yet;
The ones that cite her most
Have never passed her haunted house
Nor simplified her ghost.   20

To pity those that know her not
Is helped by the regret
That those who know her, know her less
The nearer her they get.

X

A Well

What mystery pervades a well!
The water lives so far—
Like neighbor from another world
Residing in a jar

The grass does not appear afraid,   5
I often wonder he
Can stand so close and look so bold
At what is dread to me.

Related somehow they may be,
The sedge stands next the sea—   10
Where he is floorless, yet of fear
No evidence gives he.

But nature is a stranger yet;
The ones that cite her most
Have never passed her haunted house   15
Nor simplified her ghost.

To pity those that know her not
Is helped by the regret
That those who know her, know her less
The nearer her they get.   20

1. What is lost by the omission of the second stanza? Is it
a smoother poem without this difficult quatrain? What difficulties arise within the quatrain? Discuss fear in this stanza.

2. Again the editors have corrected the poet. "Like" in line X3 is better syntactically. The editorial change in syntax turns the metaphor into a simile. "Like" makes the analogy explicit whereas the metaphor implies the analogy thus bringing the reader into active participation in the poem's development. The simile here makes less of a demand on our imaginations.

3. The editors replaced Emily Dickinson's "awe" (A12) with "dread" (X8). "Awe" had a special meaning to the poet. "Dread" may or may not be more concrete. A concrete noun evokes an *image* of something with an objective existence; a concrete illustration brings what is abstract into the range of personal, usually sensory, experience. Discuss concrete language in Dickinson's poetry.

4. Discuss rhythm, meter, and rhyme in A's fourth stanza (X's stanza 3), taking into consideration the poet's use of imperfect rhymes.

5. Does the worksheet draft betray a different vision from the one the final poem contains?

B

As imperceptibly as Grief
The Summer lapsed away—
Too imperceptibly at last
To feel like Perfidy—

A Quietness distilled—   5
As Twilight long begun—
Or Nature—Spending with Herself
Sequestered Afternoon—

Sobriety inhered
Through gaudy influence   10
The Maple lent unto the Road
And graphic Consequence

Invested sombre place—
As suddenly be worn
By sober Individual   15
A Homogeneous Gown.

Departed was the Bird—
And scarcely had the Hill—
A flower to help His straightened face
In stress of Burial   20

The Winds came closer up—
The Cricket spoke so clear
Presumption was—His Ancestors
Inherited the Floor—

The Duck drew earlier in—   25
The Morning foreign shone—
The courteous, but harrowing Grace
Of Guest who would be gone—

And thus, without a Wing
Or service of a Keel—
Our Summer made her light Escape   30
Unto the beautiful—

A

As imperceptibly as Grief
The Summer lapsed away
Too imperceptible at last
To seem like Perfidy—
A Quietness distilled   5
As Twilight long begun,
Or Nature spending with herself
Sequestered Afternoon—
The Duck drew earlier in—
The Morning foreign shone—   10
A courteous, yet harrowing Grace,

As Guest, that would be gone—
And thus, without a Wing
Or service of a Keel
Our Summer made her light escape   15
Into the Beautiful!

1. Here the two versions are two separate poems. The
omission of portions in A provides a tightness and concision
not in B. Compared to the A version, the B version seems to
have an added poem in its middle. Viewed independently,
however, do the materials of the B version cohere? Do all its
parts function toward an achieved end?

William Butler Yeats

1865—1939

The friends that have it I do wrong
Whenever I remake a song,
Should know what issue is at stake:
It is myself that I remake.

Born in Ireland, William Butler Yeats was the son of the pre-Raphaelite painter John Butler Yeats. He had no formal university education, although he did read widely. By the late 1890's, Yeats was considered a leading poet in both England and Ireland. In addition to being a poet, he was one of the leaders of the Irish Renaissance, a nationalistic movement that insisted on freedom from English domination and self-realization in all cultural aspects. He was also one of the founders of the Abbey Theatre and Senator in the Irish Free State (1922–1928). In 1923, Yeats received the Nobel Prize for literature. His writings on occultism and Irish folklore provide essential commentary on his poetry.

Any study of Yeats' poetry will reveal astonishing growth in terms of style and total performance. While the middle and late poems recall many of the concerns and habits of mind, facts of locale, and general sympathies of the very earliest poems, the changes are so great that one might doubt the same poet was at work. Growing up in the "romantic Ireland" of the late nineteenth century, Yeats had to strive to get away from personal commentaries and from an overly elaborate style, heightened to the point of extreme artificiality, which would be characterized by the terms (inadequate though they may be) "romantic agony" or romantic vagueness. Yeats' poetry grew more direct, the line "harder" and more like ordinary speech. He confronted the problems younger, exclusively twentieth-century poets were facing; that is, how can man live, or contemplate his own life, in a world that is shattered and rapidly losing all meaning? Many of his best poems have at their center a striving for some absolute or positive value that could lend a continuity and/or unity to an age in which "the center cannot hold." Throughout his poetry, the reader feels Yeats' need for a comprehensive mythology or system that would order or organize history, as well as a vision that would enable him to see his age and moment clearly. His solution, expressed in the book *A Vision*, is both personal and complex. In the poetry, the symbols, now developed and clear, remain personal though they simultaneously expand to afford meanings that are publicly available with a constant bearing on social conditions.

Yeats provides a cogent example for the modern reader's search for relevance in literature. His poetry, arising from personal experiences, nevertheless suggests, through a series of "symbolic actions," those eternal, ever current, and pressing problems that the truly alive individual faces in his social and political existence, as well as the private life of his own heart.

The "definitive" edition of Yeats' poetry is *The Collected Poems of W. B. Yeats* (New York: Macmillan, 1956). This volume contains the final versions of all the poetry that the poet wished to preserve. There is a problem in that Yeats was constantly revising his poetry, especially the early poetry, and the final version often presents a mature Yeats in the guise of an early Yeats poem. Though the final collection of poetry is beautifully organic, it does not demonstrate the total development of the poet. For a fuller awareness of the growth of his poems the reader may consult *The Variorum Edition of the Poems of W. B. Yeats* (New York: Macmillan, 1957), edited by Peter Allt and Russell K. Alspach. This great work carefully records all the revisions of the published poetry of Yeats.

Curtis B. Bradford, in *Yeats at Work* (Carbondale: Southern Illinois University Press, 1965), carries the study of Yeats' revisions one key step further. This study considers the various changes in manuscript form prior to publication. Yeats labored endlessly before he considered his poems ready for publication, and Bradford's book presents the evidence of that labor.

M. L. Rosenthal has prepared a *Selected Poems of William Butler Yeats* (New York: Macmillan, 1962), which has a fine introduction and helpful selective bibliography.

Many general statements have been made about Yeats' revisions. It is acknowledged, for example, that Yeats worked toward greater concision in his rewriting, and that he worked from prose notes. The work stands on its own and it is for each individual student to decide on the virtue or otherwise of these changes. Yeats said in 1927 that ". . . one is always cutting out the dead wood." We see this cutting process in the study of poetic revisions. Also, the changes in syntax, choice of words, rhythm, and structure indicate more than the wish to be more concise or clearer in meaning. Often the very persona behind the voice in a poem changes as the poet responds differently, at a later date, to his own experience and to the contemporary world.

For my selection of Yeats' poems, I have followed Professor Bradford's method in the handling of draft revisions. An X before a line means that Yeats canceled the whole line; revisions within a line are bracketed. Dates do not appear beneath the A versions as they are reprinted from the 1956 Macmillan edition of *The Collected Poems*. The B version dates are those of original publication.

B

A Cradle Song

The angels are bending
Above your white bed,
They weary of tending
The souls of the dead.

God smiles in high heaven   5
To see you so good;
And the old planets seven
Grow sweet with His mood.

I kiss you and kiss you,
My arms round my own;   10
Ah! how I shall miss you,
My dear, when you're grown!

                    1890

A

A Cradle Song

The angels are stooping
Above your bed;
They weary of trooping
With the whimpering dead.

God's laughing in Heaven   5
To see you so good;
The Sailing Seven
Are gay with His mood.

I sigh that kiss you,
For I must own   10
That I shall miss you
When you have grown.

   1. The early version is clearly the more romantic. While
the subject of the final poem is still romantic, the handling,
its use of language and cadence, has grown tougher, the emotion less vague. Line 11 offers illumination of this process.
   2. Words such as "bending" (B1) and "stooping" (A1)
indicate a change in attitude rather than merely a shift in

style. There is an edge to the word in the final version that determines, or foretells, other changes in the poem. While the words are close in literal meaning, they do create different images.

3. Also, "tending" (B3) and "trooping" (A3) lead to similar observations. The "trooping" angel presents a curious image. Can this abstract conception be seen concretely or realistically?

4. There is clearly no satire or irony in the early poem. Can such tones be detected in the final poem?

5. Where does Yeats change the meter or the rhythm in his revision? Note added or subtracted syllables to the measure and your own reading speed in each line.

6. In the final version, does the intentional obscurity introduced in line 7 add to or detract from the final version?

B

The Sorrow of Love

The quarrel of the sparrows in the eaves,
The full round moon and the star-laden sky,
And the loud song of the ever-singing leaves,
Had hid away earth's old and weary cry.

And then you came with those red mournful lips   5
And with you came the whole of the world's tears
And all the trouble of her labouring ships,
And all the trouble of her myriad years.

And now the sparrows warring in the eaves
The curd-pale moon, the white stars in the sky,   10
And the loud chanting of the unquiet leaves,
Are shaken with earth's old and weary cry.

                              1893

A

The Sorrow of Love

The brawling of a sparrow in the eaves,
The brilliant moon and all the milky sky,
And all that famous harmony of leaves,
Had blotted out man's image and his cry.

A girl arose that had red mournful lips   5
And seemed the greatness of the world in tears,
Doomed like Odysseus and the labouring ships
And proud as Priam murdered with his peers;

Arose, and on the instant clamorous eaves,
A climbing moon upon an empty sky,   10
And all that lamentation of the leaves,
Could but compose man's image and his cry.

1. The final version is a total rewriting of the earlier poem. How does the expression in the final poem alter the entire experience of "The Sorrow of Love"?

2. Which version is more "poetic"? This calls for a close consideration of the poet's diction. Most of Yeats' alterations lie in this area. However, is the total design or structure affected by questions of language and diction? When speaking of design and structure the first consideration is how the lines fall on the page—for example, length of stanza, length of line within each stanza. After that is settled and *felt*, other considerations arise, such as how the action or plot progresses through the verses, how the tempo and varieties of emotional content are expressed.

3. Is not "quarrel" a more melodious word than "brawling," and the idea of many sparrows quarreling a more interesting image than the image of one sparrow "brawling"? Is "brawling" more acceptable because of the new development in line 2? Or does the change to a single sparrow identify the

evolving emotions of one moved by a girl better than the possibly more exciting earlier first line? Is the poet simply gaining precision through a tightening up of his diction (viz. line 10) or is the precision an indication of a perception becoming sharper?

4. Line 3 is a substitution of a difficult and vague idea for a rather simple, yet possibly stale nineteenth-century image. In line 4 the entire vision is shifted. The language is less predictable.

5. The image in A6 is a difficult one, but announces the theme of the rest of the poem. When the image is altered in A is the theme affected? Discuss the total effect.

6. Note the repetition of "arose" in A. Does the repetition influence the total action in the poem? Note how the romantic conception in the image of B9 fulfills the action in the first line of B. Yeats replaces the image with a different figure of speech—one more difficult to translate.

7. The repetition in the last stanza follows a similar pattern in both versions. What are the differences?

8. Discuss tense in the last line of each version.

B

A Dream of Death

I dreamed that one had died in a strange place
Near no accustomed hand,
And they had nailed the boards above her face
The peasants of that land,

And wondering planted by her solitude   5
A cypress and a yew.
I came and wrote upon a cross of wood—
Man had no more to do—

'She was more beautiful than thy first love,
This lady by the trees';   10
And gazed upon the mournful stars above,
And heard the mournful breeze.

                    1891

A

A Dream of Death

I dreamed that one had died in a strange place
Near no accustomed hand;
And they had nailed the boards above her face,
The peasants of that land,
Wondering to lay her in that solitude,   5
And raised above her mound
A cross they had made out of two bits of wood,
And planted cypress round;
And left her to the indifferent stars above
Until I carved these words: 10
She was more beautiful than thy first love,
But now lies under boards.

1. The earlier version is in the ballad tradition. The ballad is conventionally a form of verse adopted for singing or recitation and primarily characterized by its presentation in simple narrative form of a dramatic or exciting episode. When the quatrains are destroyed in A, the ballad movement is altered, the tempo is faster, and the drama movement advances less by acts or stages.

2. One rhyme is done away with in A; a slant rhyme replaces it. What effect has this on the ear? The italics, used instead of quotes, affect a very different kind of change. Discuss.

3. How does the voice change in the final version? The change begins with the omission of the conjunction in A5.

How does the poet indicate a change of feeling about nature
being sympathetic to the dead lady?

D

"The great of the old times are among the Tribes of Danu,
and are kings and queens among them. Caolte was a companion of Frann; and years after his death he appeared to a
king in a forest, and was a flaming man, that he might lead
him in the darkness. When the king asked him who he was,
he said, 'I am your candlestick.' I do not remember where I
have read this story . . . Niam was a beautiful woman of the
tribes of Danu, that led Oisin to the country of the Young,
as their country is called; . . . and he came back, at last, to
bitterness and weariness."

"Knocknarea is in Sligo, and the country people say that
Maeve, still a great queen of the Western Sidhe, is buried in
the cairn of stones upon it. Clooth-na-Bare . . . went all over
the world, seeking a lake deep enough to drown her faery life,
of which she had grown weary, leaping from hill to hill, and
setting up a cairn of stones where her feet lighted, until, at
last, she found the deepest water in the world in little Lough
Ia, on the top of the bird mountain, in Sligo."

C

1

They call from the cairn on Knocknarea
They are calling calling from Knocknarea
They call from the grave of Clooth-na-Bare
And the pool [water] that is over Clooth-na-Bare
Caolte tosses his burning hair   5
But Niam murmurs 'away come away'

2

Linger no more [Why dost thou brood] where the fire burns
    bright
Filling thy heart with a mortal dream
[White Our Her] For hands wave to them [are waving] and
    eyes [are] a gleam
'Away, come away [To draw it away] to the dim twilight' 10

3

White arms glimmer and red lips are apart
If any man gaze on the Danaan band
They come between him and the deed of his hand
They come between him and the hope of his heart

4

[But come afar on their way]   15
Ah somewhere afar on their ringing way
—No hope or deed was a whit so fair
And no hope or deed is

        Manuscript version.

B

The Faery Host

The host is riding from Knocknarea
And over the grave of Clooth-na-bare,
Coulte tossing his burning hair
And Niam calling, 'away come away.'

'And brood no more where the fire is bright   5
Filling thy heart with a mortal dream,
For breasts are heaving and eyes a-gleam;
Away, come away, to the dim twilight.

'Arms are a-waving and lips apart
And if any gaze on our rushing band
We come between him and the deed of his hand,   10
We come between him and the hope of his heart.'

The host is rushing 'twixt night and day,
And where is there hope or deed as fair?
Coulte tossing his burning hair   15
And Niam calling 'away, come away.'

                                    1893

A

The Hosting of the Sidhe

The host is riding from Knocknarea
And over the grave of Clooth-na-Bare;
Caoilte tossing his burning hair,
And Niamh calling *Away, come away:*
Empty your heart of its mortal dream.   5
The winds, awaken, the leaves whirl round,
Our cheeks are pale, our hair is unbound,
Our breasts are heaving, our eyes are agleam,
Our arms are waving, our lips are apart;
And if any gaze on our rushing band,   10
We come between him and the deed of his hand,
We come between him and the hope of his heart.
The host is rushing 'twixt night and day,
And where is there hope or deed as fair?
Caoilte tossing his burning hair,   15
And Niamh calling *Away, come away.*

1. Note the change of title.
2. Again, the ballad feeling, which is primarily narrative
rather than dramatic, is replaced with a more dramatic structure. Italics replace quotation marks—an immediacy is gained.
3. Note the different use of pronoun in each version.
4. Here may be a good opportunity for "adjective" study.
"Mortal" in "mortal dream" is retained in all three versions,
while the adjectives "white" and "red" ("White arms glimmer and red lips apart") are dropped after C. Why? Maybe
"mortal" is essential to the poem's vision, while "white" and

"red" are mainly descriptive. Again, why does Yeats use so
many predicate adjectives in A?—"Our cheeks are pale,"
"Our breasts are heaving," "our eyes are agleam," and so on.

5. Does the change of the line "Filling thy heart" to
"Empty your heart" indicate a change in the poet's relation
to the call of the Fairy Band? Again, how is the poem's immediacy affected? Can we consider immediacy in itself a virtue
in poetry?

B

The Two Trees

Beloved, gaze in thine own heart,
The holy tree is growing there;
From joy the holy branches start,
And all the trembling flowers they bear.
The changing colours of its fruit   5
Have dowered the stars with merry light;
The surety of its hidden root,
Has planted quiet in the night;
The shaking of its leafy head,
Has given the waves their melody,   10
And made my lips and music wed,
Murmuring a wizard song for thee.
There, through bewildered branches, go
Winged Loves borne on in gentle strife,
Tossing and tossing to and fro   15
The flaming circle of our life.
When looking on their shaken hair,
And dreaming how they dance and dart,
Thine eyes grow full of tender care:
Beloved gaze in thine own heart.   20

Gaze no more in the bitter glass
The demons with their subtle guile,
Lift up before us as they pass,
Or only gaze a little while;

For there a fatal image grows,   25
With broken boughs and blackened leaves
And roots half hidden under snows,
Driven by a storm that ever grieves.
All things turn to barrenness
In the dim glass the demons hold—   30
The glass of outer weariness,
Made when God slept in times of old.
There, through the broken branches, go
The ravens of unresting thought;
Peering and flying to and fro,   35
To see men's souls bartered and bought.
When they are heard upon the wind,
And when they shake their wings—alas!
Thy tender eyes grow all unkind:—
Gaze no more in the bitter glass.   40

                    1892

A

The Two Trees

Beloved, gaze in thine own heart,
The holy tree is growing there;
From joy the holy branches start,
And all the trembling flowers they bear.
The changing colours of its fruit   5
Have dowered the stars with merry light;
The surety of its hidden root
Has planted quiet in the night;
The shaking of its leafy head
Has given the waves their melody,   10
And made my lips and music wed,
Murmuring a wizard song for thee.
There the Loves a circle go,
The flaming circle of our days,
Gyring, spiring to and fro   15
In those great ignorant leafy ways;
Remembering all that shaken hair

And how the wingéd sandals dart,
Thine eyes grow full of tender care:
Beloved, gaze in thine own heart.   20

Gaze no more in the bitter glass
The demons, with their subtle guile,
Lift up before us when they pass,
Or only gaze a little while;
For there a fatal image grows   25
That the stormy night receives,
Roots half hidden under snows,
Broken boughs and blackened leaves.
For all things turn to barrenness
In the dim glass the demons hold,   30
The glass of outer weariness,
Made when God slept in times of old.
There, through the broken branches, go
The ravens of unresting thought;
Flying, crying, to and fro,   35
Cruel claw and hungry throat,
Or else they stand and sniff the wind;
And shake their ragged wings; alas!
Thy tender eyes grow all unkind:
Gaze no more in the bitter glass.   40

1. In version A, line 13 introduces the image of the circle.
In the earlier version, the conception of this image is not
developed until line 16. Note the difference in vision between
the circles of version A and version B. How is our response
guided by the introduction of the circle image? Is the response
different in each case? How is the language in the poem determined by the image and the vision behind the image which
surely seeps through? Note the change in words—"gyring"
for "tossing." How is this consistent with the change of the
"circle"?

2. In version A, note the word "ignorant" in line 16. Is this
a clue to future changes in the poem? Are there any such
clues in version B?

3. There is an extension in 36A of the movement in line 35. In the earlier version a different action is suggested. Comment on how this change, which includes two lines, affects the close of the poem.

4. Note the differences in punctuation. Are they significant?

B

Cap and Bell

A Queen was loved by a jester,
And once, when the owls grew still,
He made his soul go upward
And stand on her window sill.
In a long and straight blue garment   5
It talked, ere the morn grew white.
It had grown most wise with thinking
On a foot-fall hushed and light,
But the young Queen would not listen;
She rose in her pale night-gown,   10
She drew in the brightening casement,
She snicked the brass bolts down.
He bade his heart go see her.
When the bats cried out no more:
In a garment red and quivering,   15
It sang to her through the door,
The tongue of it sweet with dreaming
On a flutter of flower-like hair;
But she took her fan from the table
And waved it out on the air.   20
'I've cap and bells,' (he pondered),
'I will send them to her and die.'
And as soon as the morn had whitened,
He left them where she went by.
She took them into her bosom,   25
In her heart she found a tune,

Her red lips sang them a love-song,
The night smelled rich with June.
She opened her door and her window,
The heart and the soul came through: 30
To her right hand came the red one,
To her left hand came the blue.
They set a noise like crickets,
A chattering wise and sweet;
And her hair was a folded flower,   35
And the quiet of love in her feet.

        1894

A

The Cap and Bells

The jester walked in the garden:
The garden had fallen still;
He bade his soul rise upward
And stand on her window-sill.

It rose in a straight blue garment,   5
When owls began to call;
It had grown wise-tongued by thinking
Of a quiet and light footfall;

But the young queen would not listen;
She rose in her pale night-gown;   10
She drew in the heavy casement
And pushed the latches down.

He bade his heart go to her,
When the owls called out no more;
In a red and quivering garment   15
It sang to her through the door.

It had grown sweet-tongued by dreaming
Of a flutter of flower-like hair;

But she took up her fan from the table
And waved it off on the air.   20

'I have cap and bells,' he pondered,
'I will send them to her and die';
And when the morning whitened
He left them where she went by.

She laid them upon her bosom,   25
Under a cloud of her hair,
And her red lips sang them a love-song
Till stars grew out of the air.

She opened her door and her window
And the heart and the soul came through,   30
To her right hand came the red one,
To her left hand came the blue.

And they set up a noise like crickets,
A chattering wise and sweet,
And her hair was a folded flower   35
And the quiet of love in her feet.

1. Discuss whether the action of this poem is more effectively expressed in the version without stanzas or in the final version.

2. In version A Yeats omits the introductory statement "A Queen was loved by a jester." What is gained by allowing the poem to imply this statement?

3. Discuss the shifts in rhythm. In your discussion consider line length and questions of stress, that is, note where the accents fall in each line and which syllable in a word is stressed. What do these considerations have to do with theme? A particular rhythm will determine the way we attend to the content.

4. Note the shifts in language. What kind of words are "brightening" in B11 and "snicked" in B12? Why did Yeats change the figure of speech in line 13? Is it merely that A13 is more direct? Why "owls" for "bats"?

5. Why is the inverted word order of B15 sacrificed for direct word order?

6. Compare stanza 7 in the final poem with line 25 and following in B. How has the quality of expression changed?

7. The last eight lines are mostly unchanged. Is the central vision of the poem implicit in these lines?

B

A rush, a sudden wheel, and hovering still
The bird descends, and her frail thighs are pressed
By the webbed toes, and that all-powerful bill
Has laid her helpless face upon his breast.
How can those terrified vague fingers push   5
The feathered glory from her loosening thighs!
All the stretched body's laid on the white rush
And feels the strange heart beating where it lies;
A shudder in the loins engenders there
The broken wall, the burning roof and tower   10
And Agamemnon dead.
                        Being so caught up,
So mastered by the brute blood of the air,
Did she put on his knowledge with his power
Before the indifferent beak could let her drop?   15

In a note published in The Dial in June 1924, Yeats wrote: "I wrote 'Leda and the Swan' because the editor of a political review asked me for a poem. I thought, 'After the individualist, demagogic movement, founded by Hobbes and popularized by the Encyclopaedists and the French Revolutions, we have a soil so exhausted that it cannot grow that crop again for centuries.' Then I thought, 'Nothing is now possible but some movement from above preceded by some violent annunciation.' My fancy began to play with Leda and the Swan for metaphor, and I began this poem; but as I wrote, bird and lady took such possession of the scene that all politics went out of it, and my friend tells me that his 'conservative readers would misunderstand the poem.' "

A

Leda and the Swan

A sudden blow: the great wings beating still
Above the staggering girl, her thighs caressed
By the dark webs, her nape caught in his bill,
He holds her helpless breast upon his breast.

How can those terrified vague fingers push   5
The feathered glory from her loosening thighs?
And how can body, laid in that white rush,
But feel the strange heart beating where it lies?

A shudder in the loins engenders there
The broken wall, the burning roof and tower   10
And Agamemnon dead.
                              Being so caught up,
So mastered by the brute blood of the air,
Did she put on his knowledge with his power
Before the indifferent beak could let her drop?   15

1. This is Yeats' only sonnet. What is he doing with this poetic form? Historically, the sonnet was a vehicle for love poetry. How does such an historical comment bear on Yeats' poem? We may consider how knowledge of the traditional sonnet structure (in this case the Italian or Petrarchan type) prepares us at least in some way for this modern poem. The Italian form is distinguished by its bipartite division into the octave and the sestet; the octave consisting of eight lines rhyming abba abba and the sestet consisting of six lines rhyming cde cde. The problem, conception, or drama introduced in the octave is resolved in the sestet. Yeats varies the form in a number of ways; for example, the rhyme scheme in the final version reads abab cdcd efg efg.

2. Is "A sudden blow" better than "A rush"? What does this distinction have to do with the poem's dramatic action?

3. The B version introduces Leda first by way of the descriptive adjective "frail." "Staggering," a very different kind

of word, is our first reference to the girl in the final poem.
Discuss.

4. A has more rhetorical questions (lines 5–10) while both
A and B have similar content. Do the questions condition our
responses? How do they prepare us for the final question of
the poem?

5. The words "strange" (line 8) and "indifferent" (line 15)
do more than describe Zeus. Discuss these words in terms of
the larger historical considerations of the poem.

6. With an eye to the sonnet's structure again, note how
the erotic drama in the first part of the poem changes to
a more meditative, rhetorical movement toward the close.
Changes in rhythm accompany this general development.

B

The Second Coming

Turning and turning in the widening gyre
The falcon can not hear the falconer;
Things fall apart; the centre can not hold;
Mere anarchy is loosed upon the world,
The blood-dimmed tide is loosed, and everywhere   5
The ceremony of innocence is drowned;
The best lack all conviction, while the worst
Are full of passionate intensity.

Surely some revelation is at hand;
Surely the Second Coming is at hand.   10
The Second Coming! Hardly are those words out
When a vast image out of *Spiritus Mundi*
Troubles my sight: a waste of desert sand;
A shape with lion body and the head of a man,
A gaze blank and pitiless as the sun,   15
Is moving its slow thighs, while all about it
Wind shadows of the indignant desert birds.

The darkness drops again but now I know
That thirty centuries of stony sleep
Were vexed to nightmare by a rocking cradle,   20
And what rough beast, its hour come round at last
Slouches towards Bethlehem to be born?

                              1920

A

The Second Coming

Turning and turning in the widening gyre
The falcon cannot hear the falconer;
Things fall apart; the centre cannot hold;
Mere anarchy is loosed upon the world,
The blood-dimmed tide is loosed, and everywhere   5
The ceremony of innocence is drowned;
The best lack all conviction, while the worst
Are full of passionate intensity.

Surely some revelation is at hand;
Surely the Second Coming is at hand.   10
The Second Coming! Hardly are those words out
When a vast image out of *Spiritus Mundi*
Troubles my sight: somewhere in sands of the desert
A shape with lion body and the head of a man,
A gaze blank and pitiless as the sun,   15
Is moving its slow thighs, while all about it
Reel shadows of the indignant desert birds.
The darkness drops again; but now I know
That twenty centuries of stony sleep
Were vexed to nightmare by a rocking cradle,   20
And what rough beast, its hour come round at last,
Slouches towards Bethlehem to be born?

    1. This poem, like many by Yeats, ends with a rhetorical
question. This device is particularly effective for poems that

contain prophecy. Prophecies are traditionally uttered in the form of riddles or mystifying questions. Discuss "The Second Coming" in terms of its final prophecy.

2. Notice the change in line 13. Is this change merely technical, that is, having to do with sound, tone, rhythm, and so on, or is the change in keeping with the poet's attempt to fully realize his original or changing vision? Even "anarchy" in the first stanza provides a clue to this line.

3. In line A17, why "reel" instead of the earlier word?

4. Note the change in line 19 from "thirty centuries" to "twenty centuries." Since the poem is a work of imaginative creation, one may consider twenty or thirty to be subject to arbitrary choice. As it happens, twenty is a very important clue to the poet's seriousness. In his work *The Vision*, Yeats theorized an historical system in which historical cycles repeat themselves every twenty centuries. The change in the later version of the poem is perhaps evidence of the poet's faithfulness to his own imagination, or else, a more accurate historical allusion to the First Coming than is in the B version.

B

Describe Byzantium as it is in the system towards the end of the first Christian millennium. A walking mummy; flames at the street corners where the soul is purified. Birds of hammered gold singing in the golden trees. In the harbour [dolphins] offering their backs to the wailing dead that they may carry them to paradise.

Transcribed from the manuscript of the 1930 Diary.

A

Byzantium

The unpurged images of day recede;
The Emperor's drunken soldiery are abed;
Night resonance recedes, night-walkers' song
After great cathedral gong;
A starlit or a moonlit dome disdains   5
All that man is,
All mere complexities,
The fury and the mire of human veins.

Before me floats an image, man or shade,
Shade more than man, more image than a shade;   10
For Hades' bobbin bound in mummy-cloth
May unwind the winding path;
A mouth that has no moisture and no breath
Breathless mouths may summon;
I hail the superhuman;   15
I call it death-in-life and life-in-death.

Miracle, bird or golden handiwork,
More miracle than bird or handiwork,
Planted on the starlit golden bough,
Can like the cocks of Hades crow,   20
Or, by the moon embittered, scorn aloud
In glory of changeless metal
Common bird or petal
And all complexities of mire or blood.

At midnight on the Emperor's pavement flit   25
Flames that no faggot feeds, nor steel has lit,
Nor storm disturbs, flames begotten of flame,
Where blood-begotten spirits come
And all complexities of fury leave,
Dying into a dance,   30
An agony of trance,
An agony of flame that cannot singe a sleeve.

Astraddle on the dolphin's mire and blood,
Spirit after spirit! The smithies break the flood,
The golden smithies of the Emperor!   35
Marbles of the dancing floor
Break bitter furies of complexity,
Those images that yet
Fresh images beget,
That dolphin-torn, that gong-tormented sea.   40

1. Often Yeats prepared a brief prose note in a notebook
or diary which would later develop into a poem. How ac-
curately does the prose note anticipate the poem?

B

The Circus Animals' Desertion

I

I sought a theme and sought for it in vain
I have sought it daily for six weeks or so
Maybe at last being but [an aged] a broken man
I must be satisfied with life although [contented with this
          heart]
Winter and summer till [this decline] old age began   5
My circus animals were all on show,
Those stilted boys, that burnished chariot,
Lion and woman and the Lord knows what.

II

X   Those images [were more grand than] outglittered life it
          seems
X   For all things counted more than life   10
X   [And every toy was] Those tragic toys were more than life
          it seems
What can I but enumerate old themes
First that sea rider Usheen led by the nose
Through three enchanted islands, allegorical dreams

Vain exaltation, battle and repose   15
A summing up of life [one of those themes] or so it seems
That might adorn old songs or courtly shows
[Or so I thought] But what cared I that set him [up] on to
        ride
I starved for the bosom of his fairy bride

III

And then a counter truth filled out its play   20
The Countess Cathleen was the name I gave it
She pity crazed had given her soul away
But masterful heaven intervened to save it
I thought my dear must her own soul destroy
So did fanaticism and hate enslave it   25
And this brought forth a dream and soon enough
The dream itself had all my thought and love

IV

And then while Fool and Blindman stole the bread
Cuchulain fought the invulnerable sea
Great mysteries there and yet when all is said   30
It was the dream itself enchanted me:
Character isolated by a deed
To engross the present and dominate memory.
The players and the painted stage took all my love
And not those things that they were emblems of.   35

V

X   Why brood upon old triumphs? Prepare to die
X   For all those burnished chariots are in flight.
X   O hours of triumph come and make me gay;
X   Even at the approach of [For even on] For on the edge of
        [the] unimagined night
X   Man has the refuge of his gaiety;   40
    But lonely to the lone; [the] tents blown away
    Women and stilts and chariots all in flight
    Man makes a refuge of his gaiety
    [Mocks the approach] Even at the approach of unimagined
        night

O hour of triumph come and make me gay
A dab of black enhances every white
Tension is but the vigour of the mind,
Cannon the god and father of mankind.   45

   Yeats reworked stanza V three more times:

                                   V

X   The faery woman, Cathleen, Fool and Blind Man
X   Their cousins and their brothers because complete
    [These processional forms] Those masterful images because
            complete
    Grew in pure [mind but out of what began?] intellect but
            how began
    [Out of] From the inanimate sweepings of the street,   5
    Bits of old newspaper, that broken can?
X   Or from old rag and bone, that raving slut
    From rag and bone, that raving slut
    Called Heart and Company. My ladder's gone
    And I lie down where all the ladders start   10
    In the foul rag and bone shop of the heart.

                                   V

    Those masterful images because complete
X   Grew in pure mind, but out of what began?
    Grew in pure intellect, but [where] from what began?
    [In this and that] [Old orange peel, dirt] Dirt, orange peel,
            the sweepings of the street
    [Bits of old] Old bits of newspaper, a broken can,   5
    Old iron, old bones, old rags, that raving slut
    Who keeps the till. Now that my ladder's gone
    I must lie down where all the ladders start
    In the foul rag and bone shop of the heart

                                   V

    And then a counter-truth filled out its play,
    The Countess Cathleen was the name I gave it;

[Dirt, orange peel] A mound of refuse or the sweepings of
     [the] a street,
Old [whiskey bottles] kettles, old bottles and a broken can
Old iron, old bones, old rags, [that] the raving slut   5
Who keeps the till. Now that my ladder's gone
I must lie down where all the ladders start
In the foul rag and bone shop of the heart.

                 1937

A

The Circus Animals' Desertion

I

I sought a theme and sought for it in vain,
I sought it daily for six weeks or so.
Maybe at last, being but a broken man,
I must be satisfied with my heart, although
Winter and summer till old age began   5
My circus animals were all on show,
Those stilted boys, that burnished chariot,
Lion and woman and the Lord knows what.

I I

What can I but enumerate old themes?
First that sea-rider Oisin led by the nose   10
Through three enchanted islands, allegorical dreams,
Vain gaiety, vain battle, vain repose,
Themes of the embittered heart, or so it seems,
That might adorn old songs or courtly shows;
But what cared I that set him on to ride,   15
I, starved for the bosom of his faery bride?

And then a counter-truth filled out its play,
The Countess Cathleen was the name I gave it;

She, pity-crazed, had given her soul away,
But masterful Heaven had intervened to save it,   20
I thought my dear must her own soul destroy,
So did fanaticism and hate enslave it,
And this brought forth a dream and soon enough
This dream itself had all my thought and love.

And when the Fool and Blind Man stole the bread   25
Cuchulain fought the ungovernable sea;
Heart-mysteries there, and yet when all is said
It was the dream itself enchanted me:
Character isolated by a deed
To engross the present and dominate memory.   30
Players and painted stage took all my love,
And not those things that they were emblems of.

III

Those masterful images became complete
Grew in pure mind, but out of what began?
A mound of refuse or the sweepings of a street,   35
Old kettles, old bottles, and a broken can,
Old iron, old bones, old rages, that raving slut
Who keeps the till. Now that my ladder's gone,
I must lie down where all the ladders start,
In the foul rag-and-bone shop of the heart.   40

1. This poem, from Yeats' *Last Poems* (1936–1939), is a
good example of his late style. One can compare it with the
first few examples of Yeats' early work and draw whatever
conclusions seem available about the poet's development and
evolution. The danger here is to assume that the later poems
are "better" merely because they are more direct, less obscure
in subject and theme. This preference may be one of modern
taste rather than a true distinction based on questions of ex-
cellences. It is always a mistake to confuse temporal progress
with true growth of poetic talent.

2. The poem is in some respects autobiographical. How do
the drafts illustrate this? How is the "poetic process" illuminated?

3. Note the different divisions of the poem. How are the major breaks like acts or scenes in drama?

4. The word "invulnerable" in B26 becomes "ungovernable" in the final version. The word in B is a direct quote from Yeats' early poem "Cuchulain's Fight with the Sea." Why would Yeats finally prefer a reference to that poem rather than a direct quote from its language?

5. Discuss the third stanza of A. Do the various draft endings illuminate the final perception? Of the material totally omitted from the final poem, what is lost and how does this loss alter the total vision?

Wilfred Owen

1893—1918

This book is not about heroes. English poetry is not yet fit to speak of them.

Nor is it about deeds, or lands, nor anything about glory, honour, might, majesty, dominion, or power, except War.

Above all I am not concerned with Poetry.

My subject is War, and the pity of War.

The Poetry is in the pity.

Yet these elegies are to this generation in no sense consolatory. They may be to the next. All a poet can do today is warn. That is why the true Poets must be truthful.

Preface to WILFRED OWEN'S
War Poems

"I was a boy when I first realized that the fullest life livable was a poet's and my later experience ratifies it."

WILFRED OWEN to his mother

WILFRED OWEN was born in Shropshire, England, in the house of his maternal grandfather, Edward Shaw. But the date and circumstances of his death are far more central to the study of his poetry. He was killed in action in World War I at the age of twenty-five while trying to get his men across a canal. The bulk of his poetry was written in the trenches between August, 1917, and September, 1918, and the brevity of his own life provides a quiet commentary to the bitter ironies and themes of death and war which make up the substance of his poetry.

The tone of modern poetry was permanently affected by the war experience. This can best be seen in the poetry of those generally neglected poets, the Trench poets of 1914–1918, among them Rupert Brooke, Siegfried Sassoon, Charles Sorley, Robert Graves, Isaac Rosenberg, and Wilfred Owen. Owen was not the only one who died young on the battlefield; an entire generation of talented young men was lost. The infinite despair generally felt by these World War I poets produced a kind of poetry that was new for the English. The poet could no longer view war as a glorious contest with national pride as emotional ballast. Intelligent man's entire approach to the human condition received a reappraisal as a result of the vast blood-letting.

It is difficult to speak of Owen as a major poet in the same sense as we would speak of Yeats or Emily Dickinson. The volume of his verses is slim, and there has long been speculation about Owen's potential had he lived longer. Nevertheless, though only four of his poems were published in his lifetime, his war poems are believed by many to be the finest of their kind in our language.

What is most characteristic of Owen's poems of war is that he emerges as an outstanding poet of peace; love of life emerges beyond the imagery of despair.

His development as a poet directly parallels his war experience. In 1914, like so many young men, he was an idealistic soldier, full of notions about the grandeur of war. Keats was his model and a "weak luxuriousness" marked his early verses. In a very short time he moved away from the comfortable niceties of nineteenth-century verse to a harsher realism. Yet he retained the sensuousness that early and late linked him to Keats.

Though the realism is marked, Owen is never merely journalistic. The power of his imagination informs the pointed observations, as in "Strange Meeting":

It seemed that out of the battle I escaped
Down some profound dull tunnel, long since scooped
Through granite which titanic wars had grained,
Yet also there encumbered sleepers groaned,
Too fast in thoughts or death to be bestirred.

The achievement of the imagination is that it carries us beyond ourselves, and the art clearly transcends the immediate personal situation, while holding on to the immediate world.

Pity is a dominant emotion in his poems, as his preface to a projected book remarks. The pity is clear in the famous poem "Greater Love":

Red lips are not so red
As the strained stones kissed by the English Dead
Kindness of Wooed and Wooer
Seems shame to their love pure.
O love, your eyes lose lure
When I behold eyes blinded in my stead!

.   .   .

Heart, you were never hot
Nor large, nor full like hearts made great with shot;
And though your hand be pale,
Paler are all which trail
Your cross through flame and hail:
Weep, you may weep, for you may touch them not.

Owen's pity is not for himself or his miserable lot, but for the general condition of misery. Thus there is no loss of urgency as the poetry moves away from private experience and remains as relevant to our present condition as it was in 1917.

Like Keats, Owen loved the sound of language. In the genesis of an individual poem we shall see simple rhyme patterns replaced by internal rhyming and stretches of assonances. This is rich poetry, finely embellished, while at the same time it is clear and hard. Discordant sounds are not a failure of the poet's ear, but echoes of war's strident music.

The changes he made in his poetry between 1914 and shortly before his death in 1918 record the poet's seriousness toward his craft, just as the staccato-like sentences in his preface record the seriousness with which he regarded war. The ironies become more concise. In many instances, the language tightens and grows more certain of its power. The poetry becomes wider in its application, less tied to the event, while remaining rooted in actions in the most fundamental way.

Most of Wilfred Owen's autographed poems are in the British Museum, and editions or manuscript drafts exist in at least five other locations. Before the *Collected Poems of Wilfred Owen*, edited by C. Day Lewis (New Directions, 1963), which contains a biographical memoir by Edmund Blunden, the available editions were Siegfried Sassoon's *Poems* (1920) and E. Blunden's *Poems* (1931). Lewis brings together all of the known textual materials in what amounts to a variorum edition, and it is to this text that I refer. No dates appear beneath the poems because most exact dates are unknown. The war poems were composed between January 1917 and November 1918 when Owen was killed. The ordering of all drafts here follows that of Lewis.

C

Anthem for Dead Youth

What passing-bells for these who die so fast?
  —Only the monstrous anger of our guns.
Let the majestic insults of their iron mouths
  Be as the requiem of their burials.
Of choristers and holy music, none;   5
  Nor any voice of mourning, save the wail
The long-drawn wail of high far-sailing shells.

What candles may we hold to light these lost?
  —Not in the hands of boys, but in their eyes
Shall shine the many flames: holy candles.   10
  Women's wide-spread arms shall be their wreaths,
And pallor of girls' cheeks shall be their palls.
  Their flowers, the tenderness of rough men's minds.
And each slow Dusk, a drawing-down of blinds.

B

Anthem for Dead Youth

What passing-bells for you who die in herds?
 —Only the monstrous anger of the guns!
 —Only the stuttering rifles' rattled words
Can patter out your hasty orisons *(prayers)*
No chants for you, nor balms, nor wreaths, nor bells,   5
 Nor any voice of mourning, save the choirs,
And long-drawn sighs of wailing shells;-
 And bugles calling for you from sad shires.

shells = funeral bells

What candles may we hold to speed you all?
 Not in the hands of boys, but in their eyes
Shall shine [the] holy lights of our goodbyes.
 The pallor of girls' brows must be your pall.
Your flowers, the tenderness of comrades' minds,
And each slow dusk, a drawing-down of blinds.

candles at coffin = mourning of loved ones left behind

> Other drafts give alternates for the word "comrades'" in
> line 13: patient/silent. In another draft an alternate to
> line 5 is: "No mockeries for them from prayers or bells."

A

Anthem for Doomed Youth

What passing-bells for these who die as cattle?
 Only the monstrous anger of the guns.
 Only the stuttering rifles' rapid rattle
Can patter out their hasty orisons.
No mockeries now for them; no prayers nor bells,   5
 Nor any voice of mourning save the choirs,—
The shrill, demented choirs of wailing shells;
 And bugles calling for them from sad shires.

no personification added alliteration

What candles may be held to speed them all?
    Not in the hands of boys, but in their eyes   10
Shall shine the holy glimmers of good-byes.
    The pallor of girls' brows shall be their pall;
Their flowers the tenderness of patient minds,
And each slow dusk a drawing-down of blinds.

1. The final version achieves greater objectivity and control than the two earlier drafts. The poet has stepped back from the action while still close enough to see and intensely feel it. In what way do we feel the poet has stepped away from the action? Note the change in line 9 and the elimination of the second person "you" throughout stanza 1.

2. The B version is more interesting than C as it shows the poet feeling his way into the final vision by discarding much that was objectionable to him in C and, too, by making use of the material in C. To what degree does C differ from A in terms of how these poems affect the reader? How are they alike?

3. The expression "die so fast" in C1 is abandoned in the B and A versions. Owen may be picking up on the deleted phrase in the opening line of the second stanza. What idea suggested in this phrase is transmitted to the final version of the second stanza?

4. Is there a shifting attitude toward religious conventions observed in the changing imagery from C to A?

5. Which poem is more realistic? Could realism be considered a value here? Note how an artful handling of language, highly contrived as in A3, can produce the necessary illusion of reality, at least in terms of sound effects.

ℰ

1

"Down the deep, darkening lanes they sang their way
To the waiting train,
And filled its doors with faces grimly gay,
And heads and shoulders white with wreath and spray,
As men's are, slain."   5

4

Will they return, to beatings of great bells,
In wild train-loads?
A few, a few, too few for drums and yells,
May walk back, silent, to their village wells,
Up half-known roads.   10

𝒟

Down the wet darkening lanes they sang their way to the
            cattle-shed
And lined the train with faces grimly gay.
Their breasts were stuck all white with wreath and spray
As men's are, dead.

The final stanzas of The Send-Off *were well established in
Owen's mind. The opening stanza, however, went through
extensive rewriting as can be seen in this draft and the two
that follow.*

C

Low-voiced through darkening lanes they sang their way to
            the cattle-shed.
    And filled the train with faces grimly gay.
Their breasts were stuck all white with wreath and spray,
            as men's are, dead.

B

Softly down darkening lanes they sang their way
And no word said.
They filled the train with faces vaguely gay
And shoulders covered all white with wreath and spray
As men's are, dead.   5

A

The Send-Off

Down the close, darkening lanes they sang their way
To the siding-shed,
And lined the train with faces grimly gay.

Their breasts were stuck all white with wreath and spray
As men's are, dead.   5

Dull porters watched them, and a casual tramp
Stood staring hard,
Sorry to miss them from the upland camp.
Then, unmoved, signals nodded, and a lamp
Winked to the guard.   10

So secretly, like wrongs hushed-up, they went.
They were not ours:
We never heard to which front these were sent.

Nor there if they yet mock what women meant
Who gave them flowers.   15

Shall they return to beatings of great bells
In wild train-loads?
A few, a few, too few for drums and yells,
May creep back, silent, to still village wells
Up half-known roads.   20

1. These many attempts to embody one central experience suggest a great deal about the relationship of the poet to that particular experience. Poetic revision here is an index not only to craftsmanship but to human experience as well.

2. The first line of these five versions or drafts demonstrates the poet's attitude toward an action and a place (*going* "down . . . *lanes*"). It is through the choice of adjectives that Owen particularizes this action, this place. I doubt that it is possible to account for the groping evident here, but some quality of the poetic process certainly is revealed.

3. In draft E, the first stanza ends with the word "slain." This is a more dramatic word than "dead" (in most cases) and too, it lines up nicely with "spray" in the line above. Finally, however, Owen chose the word "dead." The question must not be "why?" but "to what end?" Also, how are these two words different?

4. Discuss the evolution of the final stanza.

B

Last Words

"O Jesus Christ!" one fellow sighed.
And kneeled, and bowed, tho' not in prayer, and died.
    And the Bullets sang "In Vain,"
    Machine Guns chuckled "Vain,"
    Big Guns guffawed "In Vain."   5

"Father and mother!" one boy said.
Then smiled—at nothing, like a small child; being dead.
    And the Shrapnel Cloud
    Slowly gestured "Vain,"
    The falling splinters muttered "Vain."   10

"My love!" another cried, "My love, my bud!"
Then, gently lowered, his whole face kissed the mud.

And the Flares gesticulated, "Vain,"
The Shells hooted, "In Vain,"
And the Gas hissed, "In Vain."   15

A

The Last Laugh

'O Jesus Christ! I'm hit,' he said; and died.
Whether he vainly cursed, or prayed indeed,
The Bullets chirped—In vain! vain! vain!
Machine-guns chuckled,—Tut-tut! Tut-tut!
And the Big Gun guffawed.   5

Another sighed,—'O Mother, mother! Dad!'
Then smiled, at nothing, childlike, being dead.
    And the lofty Shrapnel-cloud
    Leisurely gestured,—Fool!
    And the falling splinters tittered.   10

'My Love!' one moaned. Love-languid seemed his mood,
Till, slowly lowered, his whole face kissed the mud.
    And the Bayonets' long teeth grinned;
    Rabbles of Shells hooted and groaned;
    And the Gas hissed.   15

1. This poem is an elegy but differs from that traditional
form in its use of discords and development of tone that is
more satirical than elegiac. The elegy is a sustained and
formal poem setting forth the poet's meditations upon death
or upon a grave theme. The meditation often is occasioned
by the death of a particular person, but it may be a general-
ized observation or the expression of a solemn mood. A few
famous and conventional elegies are Gray's "Elegy Written
in a Country Churchyard," Tennyson's "In Memoriam," and
Whitman's "When Lilacs Last in the Dooryard Bloom'd."

2. The "In vain" motif or refrain in B is handled like
rapid-fire. The repetition of the phrase may create a "literary"
tone in the poem. It is abandoned in the final version for a
different kind of development. Is the idea of "In vain" abandoned or changed in the final draft?

3. Owen's use of consonantal end-rhyme is related to his
use of assonance. Consonantal end-rhyme is often called half-
rhyme or slant rhyme. Note the use at the end of verses
(lines) of words in which the final consonants in the stressed
syllables agree but the vowels that precede them differ. Likewise, assonance is the resemblance or similarity between
vowels followed by different consonants in two or more
stressed syllables. Find illustrations in this poem.

4. How does the placing of lower-pitched vowels after
higher-pitched ones affect our response to the poem in
general?

5. Discuss the shortening of the last line in the final poem.

B

The Dead-Beat (TRUE, in the incidental)

He dropped, more sullenly than wearily,
   Became a lump of stench, a clot of meat,
   And none of us could kick him to his feet.
He blinked at my revolver, blearily.

He didn't seem to know a war was on,   5
   Or see or smell the bloody trench at all . . .
   Perhaps he saw the crowd at Caxton Hall,
And that is why the fellow's pluck's all gone—

Not that the Kaiser frowns imperially.
   He sees his wife, how cosily she chats;   10
   Not his blue pal there, feeding fifty rats.
Hotels he sees, improved materially;

Where ministers smile ministerially.
    Sees Punch still grinning at the Belcher bloke;
    Bairnsfather, enlarging on his little joke,   15
While Belloc prophesies of last year, serially.

We sent him down at last, he seemed so bad,
    Although a strongish chap and quite unhurt.
    Next day I heard the Doc's fat laugh: "That dirt
You sent me down last night's just died. So glad!"   20

> Against lines 13 and 16, Owen has written, "These lines
> are years old!!" Against lines 19–20, "Those are the very
> words!"

A

The Dead-Beat

He dropped,—more sullenly than wearily,
Lay stupid like a cod, heavy like meat,
And none of us could kick him to his feet;
Just blinked at my revolver, blearily;
—Didn't appear to know a war was on,   5
Or see the blasted trench at which he stared.
"I'll do 'em in," he whined. "If this hand's spared,
I'll murder them, I will."
                A low voice said,
"It's Blighty, p'raps, he sees; his pluck's all gone,   10
Dreaming of all the valiant, that aren't dead:
Bold uncles, smiling ministerially;
Maybe his brave young wife, getting her fun
In some new home, improved materially.
It's not these stiffs have crazed him; nor the Hun."   15

We sent him down at last, out of the way.
Unwounded;—stout lad, too, before that strafe.
Malingering? Stretcher-bearers winked, "Not half!"

Next day I heard the Doc.'s well-whiskied laugh:
"That scum you sent last night soon died. Hooray."   20

1. There are fewer direct references to persons and places in A than in B, fewer proper nouns. Does this make B the more realistic poem? Note that the assurance that this event is "true" is missing, and that the Doc's "very words" are changed in the final version.

2. Discuss the rhyme pattern in both versions. Note the use of consonantal rhyme in A6–7 and slant rhyme in A16–18.

3. Abandoning the use of quatrains in the final version, Owen may have been accommodating the use of dialogue and creating a faster movement. Dialogue rather than indirect discourse produces the illusion of reality. Discuss indirect discourse in B.

4. Is our attitude toward the "dead-beat" any different in the two versions?

B

He Died Smiling

Patting goodbye, his father said, "My lad,
    You'll always show the Hun a brave man's face.
    I'd rather you were dead than in disgrace.
We're proud to see you going, Jim, we're glad."

His mother whimpered, "Jim, my boy, I frets   5
    Until ye git a nice safe wound, I do."
    His sisters said: why couldn't they go too.
His brothers said they'd send him cigarettes.

For three years, once a week, they wrote the same,
    Adding, "We hope you use the Y. M. Hut."   10
    And once a day came twenty Navy Cut.
And once an hour a bullet missed its aim.

And misses teased the hunger of his brain.
    His eyes grew scorched with wincing, and his hand
    Reckless with ague. Courage leaked, like sand   15
From sandbags that have stood three years of rain.

A

*S.I.W.**

> I will to the King,
> And offer him consolation in his
> trouble,
> For that man there has set his teeth
> to die,
> And being one that hates obedience,
> Discipline, and orderliness of life,
> I cannot mourn him.
>
> W. B. YEATS

I. THE PROLOGUE

Patting good-bye, doubtless they had told the lad
He'd always show the Hun a brave man's face;
Father would sooner him dead than disgrace,—
Was proud to see him going, aye, and glad.
Perhaps his mother whimpered how she'd fret   5
Until he got a nice safe wound to nurse.
Sisters would wish girls too could shoot, charge, curse;
Brothers—would send his favourite cigarette.
Each week, month after month, they wrote the same,
Thinking him sheltered in some Y. M. Hut,   10
Because he said so, writing on his butt
Where once an hour a bullet missed its aim
And misses teased the hunger of his brain.
His eyes grew old with wincing, and his hand
Reckless with ague. Courage leaked, as sand   15
From the best sand-bags after years of rain.
But never leave, wound, fever, trench-foot, shock,
Untrapped the wretch. And death seemed still withheld
For torture of lying machinally shelled,
At the pleasure of this world's Powers who'd run amok.   20
He'd seen men shoot their hands, on night patrol.
Their people never knew. Yet they were vile.
"Death sooner than dishonour, that's the style!"
So Father said.

* Self-Inflicted Wound.

II. THE ACTION

One dawn, our wire patrol   25
Carried him. This time, Death had not missed.
We could do nothing but wipe his bleeding cough.
Could it be accident?—Rifles go off . . .
Not sniped? No. (Later they found the English ball.)

III. THE POEM

It was the reasoned crisis of his soul   30
Against more days of inescapable thrall,
Against infrangibly wired and blind trench wall
Curtained with fire, roofed in with creeping fire,
Slow grazing fire, that would not burn him whole
But kept him for death's promises and scoff,   35
And life's half-promising, and both their riling.

IV. THE EPILOGUE

With him they buried the muzzle his teeth had kissed,
And truthfully wrote the Mother, "Tim died smiling."

Alternate version of Part III:

It was the reasoned crisis of his soul.
Against the fires that would not burn him whole
But kept him for death's perjury and scoff
And life's half-promising, and both their riling.

1. The immediate drama of B is consciously exchanged for a different kind of movement. Which opening do you prefer? In which version are we more involved in the speaker's vision, in his imagination?

2. The sentiment of B7 is intensified in A7. What else happens here? Line 13 remains the same. Comment on this line of poetry.

3. The final poem extends version B to about twice the length. Discuss the poetry in A. How has the reading experience changed?

4. Comment on how the elimination of the ballad form in
the final version affects the reader's response to the poem.

B

Head to limp head, sunk-eyed wounded scanned
Yesterday's news: the casualties (typed small)
And (large) Vast Booty from our Latest Haul.
Also they read of Cheap Homes, not yet planned,
"For," said the paper, "when the war is done   5
The men's first instinct will be for their homes.
Meanwhile our need is ships, tanks, aerodromes,
It being certain war is but begun.
Peace would do wrong to our undying dead,
Our glorious sons might even regret they died   10
If we got nothing lasting in their stead
But lived on, tired and indemnified.
All will be worthy victory, which all bought.
Yet we who labour on this ancient spot
Would wrong our very selves if we forgot   15
The greatest glory will be theirs, who fought—
Who kept the nation in integrity."
NATION? The half-legged, half-lunged did not chafe
But smiled at one another curiously
Like secret men who know their secret safe.   20
(This is the thing they know and never speak—
This Nation, one by one, has fled to France
And none lay elsewhere now, save under France.)
Pictures of their broad smiles appear in sketches,
And people say, "They're happy now, poor wretches."   25

A

Smile, Smile, Smile

Head to limp head, the sunk-eyed wounded scanned
Yesterday's Mail; the casualties (typed small)
And (large) Vast Booty from our Latest Haul.
Also, they read of Cheap Homes, not yet planned
"For," said the paper, "when this war is done   5
The men's first instinct will be making homes.
Meanwhile their foremost need is aerodromes,
It being certain war has but begun.
Peace would do wrong to our undying dead,—
The sons we offered might regret they died   10
If we got nothing lasting in their stead.
We must be solidly indemnified.
Though all be worthy Victory which all bought,
We rulers sitting in this ancient spot
Would wrong our very selves if we forgot   15
The greatest glory will be theirs who fought,
Who kept this nation in integrity."
Nation?—The half-limbed readers did not chafe
But smiled at one another curiously
Like secret men who know their secret safe.   20
(This is the thing they know and never speak,
That England one by one had fled to France,
Not many elsewhere now, save under France.)
Pictures of these broad smiles appear each week,
And people in whose voice real feeling rings   25
Say: How they smile! They're happy now, poor things.

1. A number of changes occur in the use of pronouns from
B to A (line 5 and following), creating a shift in the reader's
attitude. The change in line 7 also falls in with this general
shift. What new tone is developed as a result of these changes?

2. Discuss the adjectival change in line 10. Which produces
a more consistent rhythm, consistent with either metrical pattern or development of action?

3. Discuss the shift in emphasis in line 14. How is this carried through to the end? Discuss the developing irony here.

4. In line 18, the A version is softer, smoother. B18, while richer in image, does not move as clearly into the following line. One may still prefer it, of course.

B

Dirt*

"Rear rank one pace step back. March!"
   I shouted; and inspected the Platoon.
Their necks were craned like collars stiff with starch;
   All badges glittered like the great bassoon.

Boots dubbined; rifles clean and oiled;   5
   Belts blancoed; straps—The sergeant's cane
Prodded a lad whose haversack was soiled
   With some disgraceful muddy stain.

A

Inspection

"You! What d'you mean by this?" I rapped.
"You dare come on parade like this?"
"Please, sir, it's—" " 'Old yer mouth," the sergeant snapped.
"I takes 'is name, sir?"—"Please, and then dismiss."

Some days "confined to camp" he got,   5
For being "dirty on parade."
He told me, afterwards, the damned spot
Was blood, his own. "Well, blood is dirt," I said.

---

* This version is a manuscript draft that was intended as the opening of the A version. C. Day Lewis writes, "This version then continues, in four-line stanzas, with the sense of the (A) text."

"Blood's dirt," he laughed, looking away
Far off to where his wound had bled [he'd lain and bled/
        his body had bled]   10
And almost merged for ever into clay.
"The world is washing out its stains," he said.
"It doesn't like our cheeks so red:
Young blood's its great objection.
But when we're duly white-washed [pipe-clayed], being
        dead,   15
The race will bear Field-Marshal God's inspection."

    1. Were B attached to A, as was once intended, the entire
conflict would be shifted. The dramatic movement would have
a kind of gradual introduction and too, it would be longer,
obviously. What other differences in total effect would result?
    2. Discuss the change in language between the early draft
and the final poem.
    3. Comment on the few canceled passages in the A version.

B

The Last Piece from Craiglockhart

I dreamed that Christ had fouled the big-gun gears,
And made a permanent stoppage in all bolts
And buckled, with a smile, Mausers and Colts,
And rusted every bayonet with His tears.

And there were no more bombs, of ours or Theirs.   5
So we got out, and gathering up our plunder
Of pains, and nightmares for the night, in wonder!—
Leapt the communication trench like flares.

But at the port, a man from U.S.A.
Stopped us, and said: You go right back this minute.   10
I'll follow. Christ, your miracle ain't in it,
I'll get those rifles mended by today.

A

Soldier's Dream

I dreamed kind Jesus fouled the big-gun gears;
And caused a permanent stoppage in all bolts;
And buckled with a smile Mausers and Colts;
And rusted every bayonet with His tears.

And there were no more bombs, of ours or Theirs,   5
Not even an old flint-lock, nor even a pikel.
But God was vexed, and gave all power to Michael;
And when I woke he'd seen to our repairs.

1. The basic development between B and A is away from the particular, political, geographic situation (note the title) to a more general "Soldier's Dream."

2. In A, the vision, as well as the language, is more concise, with fewer particularizing details. Note the omission of B9. Is it significant that the poet identified the dream as belonging to a soldier?

3. Both are antiwar poems, but from different perspectives. Is there a clue to perspective in the change of "made" in B2 to "caused" in A2?

4. The "kind Jesus" of A is handled differently from the "Christ" of B. The difference also establishes a dichotomy between Jesus and God. Is there such a clear dichotomy in B? How is it different?

5. There is definite irony in the word "vexed." After all, this is hardly an emotion we attribute to the Deity.

6. How would one argue for B as the superior poem?

𝐵

To My Friend

If ever I had dreamed of my dead name
High in the heart of London; unsurpassed
By Time forever; and the fugitive, Fame,
There taking a long sanctuary at last,
—I'll better that. Yea, now, I think with shame   5
How once I wished it hidd'n from its defeats
Under those holy cypresses, the same
That mourn around the quiet place of Keats.

Now rather let's be thankful there's no risk
Of gravers scoring it with hideous screed.   10
For let my gravestone be this body-disc
Which was my yoke. Inscribe no date, nor deed.
But let thy heart-beat kiss it night and day . . .
Until the name grow vague and wear away.

A later draft has the following alternate to line 11:

But let my death be memoried on this disc

On a separate folio we find the following lines:

Well, here's a meeter tombstone; and no risk
Of mason's marring it with florid ill-scored screeds.
For let my inscription be this soldier's disc.

𝐴

To My Friend

(WITH AN IDENTITY DISC)

If ever I had dreamed of my dead name
    High in the heart of London, unsurpassed
By Time for ever, and the Fugitive, Fame,
    There seeking a long sanctuary at last,—

Or if I onetime hoped to hide its shame,   5
—Shame of success, and sorrow of defeats,—
Under those holy cypresses, the same
    That shade always the quiet place of Keats,

Now rather thank I God there is no risk
    Of gravers scoring it with florid screed.   10
Let my inscription be this soldier's disc. . . .
    Wear it, sweet friend. Inscribe no date nor deed.
But may thy heart-beat kiss it, night and day,
Until the name grow blurred and fade away.

   1. The dramatic quality of the poem resides in the tension
between speaker and the silent friend. In the A version the
friend is addressed directly in line 12. We do know, from the
title at least, that the poem is meant for a particular person,
but the expression "sweet friend" in A draws us into the situation more directly.
   2. The middle quatrain in A presents a different tone and
development of the idea than B. The contextual shift is accom-
panied by a typographical one. Comment on the use of typography. Draw from other poets as well.
   3. Line 11 has three versions. None of the choices seems
particularly successful. What is the difficulty with this line?

B

1914

War broke: and now the Winter of the world
With perishing great darkness closes in.
The cyclone of the pressure on Berlin
Is over all the width of Europe whirled,
Rending the sails of progress. Rent or furled   5
Are all Art's ensigns. Verse wails. Now begin
Famines of thought and feeling. Love's wine's thin.
The grain of earth's great autumn rots, down-hurled.

For after Spring had bloomed in early Greece,
And Summer blazed to perfect strength   10
There fell a slow grand age, a harvest home,
Quiet ripening, [rich with all increase.]
But now the exigent winter and the need
Of sowings for new Spring, and blood for seed.

urgent. pressing

𝒜

1914

War broke: and now the Winter of the world
With perishing great darkness closes in.
The foul tornado, centered at Berlin,
Is over all the width of Europe whirled,
Rending the sails of progress. Rent or furled   5
Are all Art's ensigns. Verse wails. Now begin
Famines of thought and feeling. Love's wine's thin.
The grain of human Autumn rots, down-hurled.

For after Spring had bloomed in early Greece,
And Summer blazed her glory out with Rome,   10
An Autumn softly fell, a harvest home,
A slow grand age, and rich with all increase.
But now, for us, wild Winter, and the need
Of sowings for new Spring, and blood for seed.

1. The two versions of the third line are developed with
different language, yet the same idea is developed. The change
in line 8, however, while clearly a rhythmic change, also offers
a shift in emphasis.

2. The second stanza of B is particularly rough in comparison with the final version. Words are used differently in the
earlier draft. Note the particular use of "blazed." Line 13 in
B is a difficult line to read aloud. In the corrected version, the
line is smoother and more consistent with the developing
theme.

�

W. H. Auden

1907—

Before emigrating to the United States from England in 1939, Wystan Hugh Auden taught school and was a leading figure of the socially conscious left-oriented poetry movement of the 1930's with other poets such as Stephen Spender, C. Day Lewis, and Louis MacNeice. Now an American citizen, his poetry and the revisions of earlier poems reveal a more conservative position than his earlier, more widely known poetry. Joseph Warren Beach's *The Making of the Auden Canon* (1957) is a valuable study of the poet and his revisions.

In the late 1930's, Auden moved from a left-wing political faith to orthodox Christianity, and critics have made much of the shift in his poetry around that time. The reader must watch the changes closely before generalizing about the overall pattern of development in Auden's poetry. Auden has maintained that there is no easy or definitive line of development, and in at least one edition, *Collected Poems* (1945), the poems have been printed in a nonchronological arrangement deliberately in order to prevent any such tracing of a course. But readers generally enjoy tracing courses, however meaningful or however irrelevant the activity. The poems here are chronologically arranged.

Auden has written a great deal of light verse, and although not represented in this text, the tone and feelings of his light verse are present in many of the serious and morally instructive poems. Growing out of the tradition of social protest poetry, much of the poetry not in this genre of light verse has the shared motivation of poetry of instruction—though it is rarely didactic or propagandistic. The poetry is engaged in confrontation with the poet's own self, an activity that allows the most socially conscious poetry a private, or at least nonpublic, aspect.

Auden is constantly revising his poems. Basically, the reasons for the changes have to do with aesthetics. The poet is always aiming at a better-made work of art, and questions of political, social, and religious ideology are secondary. Often these changes, technical and stylistic, social and political, occur in the same poem and the reader need not bother to point to one and say, "this change is because the poet has changed politically," but rather, "in this revision the poet is trying to approximate his altered vision which, indeed, includes art as well as social considerations."

In the foreword to the 1967 edition of *Collected Shorter Poems 1927–1957*, which is chronologically arranged, Auden states his dislike for dishonest poetry, or dishonest language in his earlier poems. Through the process of revision he is stripping his poetry of what he considers "rhetorically effective" yet untrue, untrue to his own experience or belief. The reader must be aware that when one changes his beliefs after many years he often will suspect earlier phrases of being dishonest as they do not represent current beliefs. Thus we read Auden's preface on his revisions with extreme care, perhaps even with skepticism. He writes, ". . . I have never, consciously at any rate, attempted to revise my former thoughts or feelings, only the language in which they were first expressed, when on further consideration, it seemed to me inaccurate, lifeless, prolix, or painful to the ear."

The presentation of the poems in this chapter differs from the rest of the book in general, in that at times I present only the final version in its entirety. The bracketed words are earlier variants that were replaced in the final version by the underlined words. Unless otherwise noted, all A versions are taken from the 1945 *Collected Poetry* and/or the 1967 *Collected Shorter Poems* (these two volumes contain many identical poems). When the B version is from *Collected Poetry* and the A version from *Collected Shorter Poems*, it is noted as such beneath the poems.

A

Taller To-day

Taller to-day, we remember similar evenings,
Walking together in a windless orchard
Where the brook runs over the gravel, far from the glacier.

Nights come bringing the snow, and the dead howl
Under [the] headlands in their windy dwelling   5
Because the Adversary put too easy questions
On the lonely roads.

But happy now, though no nearer each other,
We see [the] farms lighted all along the valley;
Down at the mill-shed hammering stops   10
And men go home.

Noises at dawn will bring
Freedom for some, but not this peace
No bird can contradict; <u>passing but here</u>, [passing, but is]
       sufficient now
For something fulfilled this hour, loved or endured.   15

        The bracketed words above and additional stanzas below
        are from a version published in *Poems* (1930).

Between stanzas 1 and 2:

Again in the room with the sofa hiding the grate,
Look down to the river when the rain is over,
See him turn to the window, hearing our last
Of Captain Ferguson.

It is seen how excellent hands have turned to commonness.
One staring too long, went blind in a tower,
One sold all his manors to fight, broke through, and faltered.

   1. There is specific detail in the several lines omitted from
the A version. How are these lines different from the rest of

the poem? A possible answer is that they are obscure in a way that nothing in the final version is obscure. This is an obscurity of allusion. Whatever difficulty the final version may offer, it is not one of literary or personal allusions.

2. The deletion of the article in lines 5 and 9 gives these lines a toughness, a masculinity they did not earlier have. Can you explain why? (Reading aloud helps.)

A

Consider

Consider this and in our time
As the hawk sees it or the helmeted airman:
The clouds rift suddenly—look there
At cigarette-end smouldering on a border
At the first garden party of the year.   5
Pass on, admire the view of the massif
Through plate-glass windows of the Sport Hotel;
Join there the insufficient units
Dangerous, easy, in furs, in uniform,
And constellated at reserved tables,   10
Supplied with feelings by an efficient band,
Relayed elsewhere to farmers and their dogs
Sitting in kitchens in the stormy fens.

Long ago, supreme Antagonist,
More powerful than the great northern whale,   15
Ancient and sorry at life's limiting defect,
In Cornwall, Mendip, or the Pennine moor
Your comments on the highborn mining-captains,
Found they no answer, made them wish to die
—Lie since in barrows out of harm.   20
You talk to your admirers every day
By stilted harbours, derelict works,
In strangled orchards, and a silent comb

Where dogs have worried or a bird was shot.
Order the ill that they attack at once: 25
Visit the ports and, interrupting
The leisurely conversation in the bar
Within a stone's throw of the sunlit water,
Beckon your chosen out. Summon
Those handsome and diseased youngsters, those women   30
Your solitary agents in the country parishes;
And mobilize the powerful forces latent
In soils that make the farmer brutal
In the infected sinus, and the eyes of stoats.
Then, ready, start your rumour, soft   35
But horrifying in its capacity to disgust
Which, spreading magnified, shall come to be
A polar peril, a prodigious alarm,
Scattering the people, as torn-up paper
Rags and utensils in a sudden gust,   40
Seized with immeasurable neurotic dread.

Seekers after happiness, all who follow
The convolutions of your simple wish,
It is later than you think; nearer that day
Far other than that distant afternoon   45
Amid rustle of frocks and stamping feet
They gave the prizes to the ruined boys.
You cannot be away, then, no
Not though you pack to leave within an hour,
Escaping humming down arterial roads: 50
The date was yours; the prey to fugues,
Irregular breathing and alternate ascendancies
After some haunted migratory years
To disintegrate on an instant in the explosion of mania
Or lapse for ever into a classic fatigue.   55

   Between lines 41 and 42:
Financier, leaving your little room
Where money is made but not spent,
You'll need your typist and your boy no more;
The game is up for you and for the others,

Who, thinking, pace in slippers on the lawns
Of College Quad or Cathedral Close,
Who are born nurses, who live in shorts
Sleeping with people and playing fives.

1. Beginning with line 42, Auden is speaking to the financier, confronting him with all the weight of the warnings
implied in the poem up to that point. The allusions have been
topical as well as universal. The imagery is suggestive rather
than direct and the didactic turn of the poem is everywhere
muted by this suggestiveness of language.

2. The omitted lines contain an even more direct confrontation, not with the reader but with a particular social type.
Surely the poem builds in its rhetoric, its frequent violent
images, toward the specific social comment. Without the lines
the poet later deleted, the "you" in line 49 becomes a more
general "you" and the reader is drawn in, in a way unlikely
in the earlier version.

3. What is it about the tone in the omitted material that
Auden may have found unacceptable at the time of revision?
Does one regret the omission of colloquial constructions such
as "the game is up" that appear in the missing stanza?

$\mathcal{A}$

No Change of Place

Who will endure
Heat of day and winter danger,
Journey from one place to another,
Nor be content to lie
Till evening upon headland over bay,   5
Between the land and sea
Or smoking wait till hour of food,
Leaning on chained-up gate
At edge of wood?

Metals run,   10
Burnished or rusty in the sun,
From town to town,
And signals all along are down;
Yet nothing passes
But envelopes between these places,   15
Snatched at the gate and panting read indoors,
And first spring flowers arriving smashed,
Disaster stammered over wires,
And pity flashed.

For should professional traveller come,   20
Asked at the fireside, he is dumb,
Declining with a <u>secret</u> [small mad] smile,
And all the while
Conjectures on <u>our maps grow stranger</u> [the maps that lie
          About in ships long high and dry Grow stranger
          and stranger.]

<u>And threaten danger.</u>   25
There is no change of place:
No one will ever know
For what conversion brilliant capital is waiting,
What ugly feast may village band be celebrating;
For no one goes   30
Further than railhead or the ends of piers,
Will neither go nor send his son
Further through foothills than the rotting stack
Where gaitered gamekeeper with dog and gun
Will shout 'Turn Back.'   35

          The bracketed words above and the additional lines be-
          low are from a version published in *Poems* (1930).

  Between lines 26 and 27:

But shifting of the head
To keep off glare of lamp from face,
Or climbing over to wall-side of bed;

1. The three lines omitted from the final version provide a realistic and somewhat dramatic note to the stanza. Consider whether Auden may have taken them out in order to direct attention in the stanza to the final action, the image of the "gamekeeper with dog and gun . . ." Do you feel there is a loss as a result of the omission?

2. Note the use of half-rhymes in both versions.

3. The changes between lines 20 and 25 are of rhythm and tone as well as development of theme. A "secret smile" communicates what different idea from a "small mad smile"? Both images grow out of the central theme of prophecy in the poem.

4. Have you noted a similarity in voice and statement in the first three poems?

A

Through the Looking Glass

Earth has turned [The earth turns] over; our side feels
      the cold,
And life sinks choking in the wells of trees,
A faint heart here and there stops ticking, [The ticking
      heart comes to a standstill,] killed,
Icing on ponds entrances village [The icing on the pond
      waits for the] boys:
Among wreathed [the] holly and wrapped [the] gifts I
      move,   5
Old [The] carols on the piano, a [the] glowing hearth,
All our traditional sympathy with birth,
Put by your challenge to the shifts of love.

Your portrait hangs before me on the wall
And there what view I wish for I shall find,   10
The wooded or the stony, though not all
The painter's gifts can make its flatness round;

Through each blue iris [the blue irises] greet the heaven
        of failures,
That [The] mirror world would where Logic is reversed,
Where age becomes the handsome child at last,   15
The glass wave [sea] parted for the country sailors.

There [Where] move the enormous comics, drawn from
        life—
My father as an Airedale and a gardener,
My mother chasing letters with a knife:
You are not present as a character;   20
(Only the family have speaking parts)
You are a valley or a river-bend,
The one an aunt refers to as a friend,
The tree from which the weasel racing starts.

Behind me roars the other [False; but no falser than the]
        world it matches,   25
Love's daytime kingdom which I say you rule,
His [The] total state where all must wear your badges,
Keep order perfect as a naval school:
Noble emotions, organized and massed,
Line the straight flood-lit tracks of memory   30
To cheer your image as it flashes by,
All lust at once informed on and suppressed.

Yours is the only name expressive there,
And family affection speaks [the one] in cypher,
Lay-out of hospital and street and square   35
That comfort to the homesick children offer,
As I, their author, stand between these dreams,
Unable to choose either for a home, [Son of a nurse and
        doctor, loaned a dream,]
Your would-be lover who has never come
In a [the] great bed at midnight to your arms.   40
Such dreams are amorous; they are indeed:
But no one but myself is loved in these,
While [And] time flies on above the dreamer's head,
Flies on, flies on, and with your beauty flies,

And pride succeeds to each succeeding state, [All things
                he takes and loses but conceit,]   45
Still able to buy up [The Alec who can buy] the life within,
License no liberty except his own,
Order the fireworks after the defeat.

Language of moderation cannot hide:—
My sea is empty and the waves are rough,   50
Gone from the map the shore where childhood played,
Tight-fisted as a peasant, eating love;
Lost in my wake the archipelago,
Islands of self through which I sailed all day,
Planting a pirate's flag, a generous boy;   55
And lost my [the] way to action and to you.

Lost if I steer. Tempest and tide [Gale of desire] may blow
Sailor and ship past the illusive reef,
And I yet land to celebrate with you
The birth of [a] natural order and true [of] love: 60
With you enjoy the untransfigured scene,
My father down the garden in his gaiters,
My mother at her bureau writing letters,
Free to our favours, all our titles gone.

> *Collected Shorter Poems* (1967)
>
> The bracketed words are from a version published in
> *Look, Stranger* (1936).
> The 1945 *Collected Poetry* version of this poem is
> identical to the A version presented here with the follow-
> ing two exceptions: l. 7: our/on, l. 13: greet/see.

1. While the major action of the poem is in the present, the
first change shifts one action to the past. How does this affect
the meaning and therefore the poem's tone?

2. Discuss tonal change in line 3, making note of the additional adjective and the casual air. The adding on of adjectives
in line 5 demonstrates the poet making his vision more specific. Is the vision clearer in both of these instances?

3. Discuss the change in idea in line 25, and how this change from statement to image alters our reading of the entire stanza.

4. A number of the changes include the poet as actor or player; other shifts in language seem to shift his role in the action (line 38).

5. Though "gale of desire" may sound "poetical" (line 57), it may be a cliché. Discuss clichés and their effect on language.

A

A Summer Night

(TO GEOFFREY HOYLAND)

Out on the lawn I lie in bed,
Vega conspicuous overhead
   In the windless nights of June,
As congregated leaves [Forests of green have done] complete
Their day's activity; my feet   5
   Point to the rising moon.

Lucky, this point in time and space
Is chosen as my working-place,
   Where the sexy airs of summer,
The bathing hours and the bare arms,   10
The leisured drives through a land of farms
   Are good to a newcomer.

Equal with colleagues in a ring
I sit on each calm evening
   Enchanted as the flowers   15
The opening light draws out of hiding
With all its gradual dove-like pleading,
   Its logic and its powers:

That later we, though parted then,
May still recall these evenings when   20
    Fear gave his watch no look;
The lion griefs loped from the shade
And on our knees their muzzles laid,
    And Death put down his book.

Now north and south and east and west   25
Those I love lie down to rest;
    The moon looks on them all,
The healers and the brilliant talkers
The eccentrics and the silent walkers,
    The dumpy and the tall.   30

She climbs the European sky,
Churches and power-stations lie
    Alike among earth's fixtures:
Into the galleries she peers
And blankly as a butcher [an orphan] stares   35
    Upon the marvellous pictures.

To gravity attentive, she
Can notice nothing here, though we
    Whom hunger does not [cannot] move,
From gardens where we feel secure   40
Look up and with a sigh endure
    The tyrannies of love:

And, gentle, do not care to know,
Where Poland draws her eastern bow,
    What violence is done,   45
Nor ask what doubtful act allows
Our freedom in this English house,
    Our picnics in the sun.

Soon, soon, through [Soon through the] dykes of our content
The crumbling flood will force a rent   50
    And, taller than a tree,
Hold sudden death before our eyes

Whose river dreams long hid the size
   And vigours of the sea.

But when the waters make retreat   55
And through the black mud first the wheat
   In shy green stalks appears,
When stranded monsters gasping lie,
And sounds of riveting terrify
   Their whorled unsubtle ears,   60

May these delights [this for which] we dread to lose,
This [Our] privacy, need no excuse
   But to that strength belong,
As through a child's rash happy cries
The drowned parental voices [voice of his parents] rise   65
   In unlamenting song.

After discharges of alarm
All unpredicted let them [may it] calm
   The pulse of nervous nations,
Forgive the murderer in his glass,   70
Tough in their [its] patience to surpass
   The tigress her swift motions.

         The bracketed words above and additional stanzas below
         are from a version published in *Look, Stranger* (1936).

   Between stanzas 4 and 5:
Moreover, eyes in which I learn
That I am glad to look, return
   My glances every day;
And when the birds and rising sun
Waken me, I shall speak with one
   Who has not gone away.

   Between stanzas 8 and 9:
The creepered wall stands up to hide
The gathering multitude outside
   Whose glances hunger worsens;

Concealing from their wretchedness
Our metaphysical distress,
    Our kindness to ten persons.

And now no path on which we move
But shows already traces of
    Intentions not our own,
Thoroughly able to achieve
What our excitement could conceive,
    But our hands left alone.

For what by nature and by training
We loved, has little strength remaining:
    Though we would gladly give
The Oxford colleges, Big Ben,
And all the birds in Wicken Fen,
    It has no wish to live.

> The A version here is taken from the 1967 edition of
> *Collected Shorter Poems.* In the 1945 edition of *Collected
> Poetry,* the poem is titled "A Summer Night 1933." It is
> otherwise identical to the A version presented here.

1. Benjamin Britten set this poem (stanzas 1, 5, 7, and 8 of the *Collected Poetry* version) to music. The simple mood of the composition has been termed "detached foreboding." What kind of thoughts does "detached foreboding" provoke and are they applicable to this poem?

2. Here the poet accomplishes a deliberate distancing of his material—the moon is looking down upon "them all," which includes the large European landscape and individuals as well. The voice of this poem is equivalent to the moon's eye view: it is a distant voice, though it is the poet's very own, talking ironically or bitterly (view change in line 35), yet at the same time responsive to the scene in that he not only observes, but feels.

3. The distant perspective of the moon's view of the European landscape is paralleled by the voice of the poet's own applied emotional distance from the scene he is no doubt car-

ing about. Note how he locates himself specifically, from the opening line, in time and place. Line 35 contains an even cooler metaphor than in the earlier version and suddenly such a word as "marvelous" in the following line seems more ironic. Explain how this works.

4. In line 4 the change is from an explicit image to one less explicit but still pictorial. The word "congregated" contains suggestions that transcend the imagery itself.

5. Do the changes and major omissions change the voice of the poem? Is there a tone in any of the omitted material that Auden may have felt ran counter to the tone of the new poem? For example, there is a personal note in the stanza earlier included between stanzas 4 and 5 that is hardly present in the rest of the poem.

6. The single changes in stanzas 6 and 7 shift the tone and the point of view in both stanzas. Are these shifts represented elsewhere in the poem?

7. Auden is a master of the colloquial tone of voice, yet with the changes in stanzas 9 and 11 the poetry becomes more formal, and emphatic.

8. What is it about the content of the three stanzas which stood between 8 and 9 that prompted Auden to delete them? What is missed in them?

B

Journey to Iceland

And the traveller hopes: "Let me be far from any
Physician"; and the ports have names for the sea,
    The citiless, the corroding, the sorrow;
    And North means to all: "Reject."

And the great plains are forever where the cold fish is
       hunted   5
And everywhere: the light birds flicker and flaunt:
    Under the scolding flag the lover
    Of islands may see at last,

Faintly, his limited hope: <u>and</u> [as] he nears the glitter
Of glaciers, the sterile immature mountains intense   10
    In the abnormal day of this world, and a river's
    Fan-like polyp of sand.

Then let the good citizen here find natural marvels:
A horse-shoe ravine, an issue of steam from a cleft
    In the rock, and rocks, and waterfalls brushing the   15
    Rocks, and among the rocks birds.

And the student of prose and conduct places to visit:
The site of a church where a bishop was put in a bag,
    The bath of a great historian, the <u>rock</u> [fort] where
    An outlaw dreaded the dark;   20

Remember the doomed man thrown by his horse and crying,
"Beautiful is the hillside, I will not go,"
    The old woman confessing, "He that I loved the
    Best, to him I was the worst."

For Europe is absent: this is an island and therefore   25
<u>Unreal. And the steadfast</u> [A refuge, where the fast]
      affections of its dead may be bought
    By those whose dreams accuse them of being
    Spitefully alive, and the pale

From too much passion of kissing feel pure in its deserts.
Can they? For the world is, and the present, and the lie.   30
    The narrow bridge over the torrent,
    And the small farm under the crag

Are the natural setting for the jealousies of a province;
And the weak vow of fidelity is formed by the cairn;
    And within the indigenous figure on horseback   35
    On the bridle path down by the lake

The blood moves also by crooked and furtive inches,
Asks all <u>your</u> [our] questions: "Where is the homage? When
    Shall justice be done? O who is against me?
    Why am I always alone?"   40

[Present then the world to the world with its mendicant
      shadow;
Let the suits be flash, the Minister of Commerce insane;
    Let jazz be bestowed on the huts, and the beauty's
    Set cosmopolitan smile.]

For [No,] our time has no favourite suburb; no local
      features   45
Are those of the young for whom all wish to care;
    The promise is only a promise, the fabulous
    Country impartially far.

Tears fall in all the rivers. Again the driver
Pulls on his gloves and in a blinding snowstorm starts   50
    Upon his deadly journey, and again the writer
    Runs howling to his art.

       Letters from Iceland (1937)

    *In a letter to Christopher Isherwood, Auden writes: "No,
you were wrong. I did not write: 'the ports have names for
the sea' but 'the poets have names for the sea.' However, as so
often before, the mistake seems better than the original idea,
so I'll leave it."* (Letters from Iceland [*1937*])

A

Journey to Iceland

Each traveller prays Let me be far from any
physician, every port has its name for the sea,
    the citiless, the corroding, the sorrow,
      and North means to all Reject.

These plains are for ever where cold creatures are hunted   5
and on all sides: white wings flicker and flaunt;
    under a scolding flag the lover
      of islands may see at last,

in outline, his limited hope, as he nears a glitter
of glacier, sterile immature mountains intense   10
   in the abnormal northern day, and a river's
      fan-like polyp of sand.

Here let the citizen, then, find natural marvels,
a horse-shoe ravine, an issue of steam from a cleft
   in the rock, and rocks, and waterfalls brushing   15
      the rocks, and among the rocks birds;

the student of prose and conduct places to visit,
the site of a church where a bishop was put in a bag,
   the bath of a great historian, the fort where
      an outlaw dreaded the dark,   20

remember the doomed man thrown by his horse and crying
Beautiful is the hillside. I will not go,
   the old woman confessing He that I loved the
      best, to him I was the worst.

Europe is absent: this is an island and should be   25
a refuge, where the affections of its dead can be bought
   by those whose dreams accuse them of being
      spitefully alive, and the pale

from too much passion of kissing feel pure in its deserts.
But is it, can they, as the world is and can lie?   30
   A narrow bridge over a torrent,
      a small farm under a crag

are natural settings for the jealousies of a province:
a weak vow of fidelity is made at a cairn,
   within the indigenous figure on horseback   35
      on the bridle-path down by the lake

his blood moves also by furtive and crooked inches,
asks all our questions: Where is the homage? When
   shall justice be done? Who is against me?
      Why am I always alone?   40

Our time has no favourite suburb, no local features
are those of the young for whom all wish to care;
    its promise is only a promise, the fabulous
        country impartially far.

Tears fall in all the rivers: again some driver   45
pulls on his gloves and in a blinding snowstorm starts
    upon a fatal journey, again some writer
        runs howling to his art.

1. Auden, here and elsewhere, is lamenting or prophesying
the doom of both England and Western society. Prophecy remains, despite an affected casualness of tone, in both versions.
This does not communicate a coolness of concern. Rather,
Auden's personna, his assumed voice, is a device used to
implement tension.
2. Has the poet disturbed the sense of "realism" or veri-
similitude by eliminating the quote?
3. Discuss the change in rhythm and tone in the first two
stanzas. Does the use of the conjunction "And" in B5 alter
rhythm, tone, and meaning?
4. There are many changes of single words, for example,
"hopes" to "prays" in the first line, which indicate a change
in attitude or sensibility. How then does the pattern affect the
entire poem as an object of art?

A

Herman Melville

(FOR LINCOLN KIRSTEIN)

Towards the end he sailed into an extraordinary mildness,
And anchored in his home [at last] and reached his wife
And rode within the harbour of her hand,

And went across each morning to an office
As though his occupation were another island.   5

Goodness existed: that was the new knowledge.
His terror had to blow itself quite out
To let him see it; but it was the gale had blown him
Past the Cape Horn of sensible success
Which [That] cries: 'This rock is Eden. Shipwreck here.'   10
[And like an instinct had said always "No,"]

But deafened him with thunder and confused with lightning:
—The maniac hero hunting like a jewel
The rare ambiguous monster that had maimed his sex,
Hatred for hatred ending in a scream,
The unexplained survivor breaking off the nightmare—   15
All that was intricate and false; the truth was simple.

Evil is unspectacular and [formidable but] always human,
And shares our bed and eats at our own table,
And we are introduced to Goodness every day,
Even in drawing-rooms among a crowd of faults;   20
He has a name like Billy and is almost perfect,
But wears a stammer like a decoration:
And every time they meet the same thing has to happen;
It is the Evil that is helpless like a lover
And has to pick a quarrel and succeeds,   25
And both are openly destroyed before our eyes.

For now he was awake and knew
No one is ever spared except in dreams;
But there was something else the nightmare had distorted—
Even the punishment was human and a form of love: 30
[And he himself had never been abandoned;]
The howling storm had been his father's presence
And all the time [way] he had been carried on his father's
            breast.
Who now had set him gently down and left him.
He stood upon the narrow balcony and listened:
And all the stars [night] above him sang as in his
            childhood   35

'All, all is vanity,' but it was not the same;
For now the words descended like the calm of mountains—
—Nathaniel had been shy because his love was selfish—
Reborn, he cried in exultation and surrender
'The Godhead is broken like bread. We are the pieces.'   40

And sat down at his desk and wrote a story.

> The bracketed words are from a version published in the
> *Southern Review*, V, 2 (1939).

1. In the portrait poem, of which a few are reprinted here,
Auden's tone is less vindictive and doomful than in the social-
political poems of the early 1930's. Such a shift as we see in
line 17 indicates a softening of voice. The fourth stanza is also
a good example of a lightening of tone. It is rich, as is the
entire poem, in metaphor and possesses a rather carefully
balanced rhetorical manner.
2. The language is made more precise where there are
minor changes. Comment on the lines omitted.
3. Do we know more about Melville than before? Do we
know more about Auden? It has been suggested that these
portraits provide a particular kind of literary criticism.

✲

B

At the Grave of Henry James

The snow, less intransigeant than their marble,
Has left the defence of whiteness to these tombs;
    For all the pools at my feet
Accommodate blue now, and echo such clouds as occur
To the sky, and whatever bird or mourner the passing   5
    Moment remarks they repeat *(In A)*

While [the] rocks, named after singular spaces
Within which images wandered once that caused
    All to tremble and offend,
Stand here in an innocent stillness, each marking the spot   10
Where one more series of errors lost its uniqueness
    And novelty came to an end.

worlds

To whose real advantage were such transactions,
When (words) of reflection were exchanged for trees?
    What living occasion can   15
Be just to the absent? [O] noon but reflects on itself,
And the small taciturn stone, that is the only witness
    To a great and talkative man,

Has no more judgment than my ignorant shadow
Of odious comparisons or distant clocks   20
    Which challenge and interfere
With the heart's instantaneous reading of time, time that is
A warm enigma no longer in you for whom I
    Surrender my private cheer,

Startling the awkward footsteps of my apprehension,   25
The flushed assault of your recognition is
    The donnée of this doubtful hour:
O stern proconsul of intractable provinces,
O poet of the difficult, dear addicted artist,
    Assent to my soil and flower.   30

As I stand awake on our solar fabric,
That primary machine, the earth, which gendarmes, banks,
    And aspirin pre-suppose.
On which the clumsy and sad may all sit down, and any
            who will
Say their a-ha to the beautiful, the common locus   35
    Of the master and the rose.

Our theatre, scaffold, and erotic city
Where all the infirm species are partners in the act
    Of encroachment bodies crave,

Though solicitude in death is de rigueur for their flesh   40
And the self-denying hermit flies as it approaches
   Like the carnivore to a cave.

That its plural numbers may unite in meaning,
Its vulgar tongues unravel the knotted mass
   Of the improperly conjunct,   45
Open my eyes now to all its hinted significant forms,
Sharpen my ears to detect amid its brilliant uproar
   The low thud of the defunct.

O dwell, ironic at my living centre,
Half ancestor, half child; because the actual self   50
   Round whom time revolves so fast
Is so afraid of what its motions might possibly do
That the actor is never there when his really important
   Acts happen. Only the past

Is present, no one about but the dead as,   55
Equipped with a few inherited odds and ends,
   One after another we are
Fired into life to seek that unseen target where all
Our equivocal judgments are judged and resolved in
   One whole <u>Alas or Hurrah</u>. [alas or hurrah]   60

And only the unborn <u>remark</u> [mark] the disaster
When, though it makes no difference to the pretty airs
   The bird of Appetite sings,
And Amour Propre is his usual amusing self,
Out from the jungle of an undistinguished moment   65
   The flexible <u>shadow</u> [Shadow] springs.

Now more than ever, when torches and snare-drum
Excite the squat women of the saurian brain
   Till a milling mob of fears
Breaks in insultingly on anywhere, when in our dreams   70
Pigs play on the organs and the blue sky runs shrieking
   As the Crack of Doom appears,

Are the good ghosts needed with the white magic
Of their subtle loves. War has no ambiguities
    Like a marriage; the result   75
Required of its affaire fatale is simple and sad,
The physical removal of all human objects
    That conceal the Difficult.

Then remember me that I may remember
The test we have to learn to shudder for is not   80
    An historical event,
That neither the low democracy of a nightmare nor
An army's primitive tidiness may deceive me
    About our predicament.

That catastrophic situation which neither   85
Victory nor defeat can annul; to be
    Deaf yet determined to sing,
To be lame and blind yet burning for the Great Good Place,
To be radically [essentially] corrupt yet mournfully attracted
    By the Real Distinguished Thing.   90

And shall I not specially bless you as, vexed with
My little inferior questions, today I stand
    Beside the bed where you rest
Who opened such passionate arms to your Bon when It
    [it] ran
Towards you with its overwhelming reasons pleading   95
    All beautifully in Its [its] breast?

O with what innocence your hand submitted
To these [those] formal rules that help a child to play,
    While your heart, fastidious as
A delicate nun, remained true to the rare noblesse   100
Of your lucid gift and, for its own sake, ignored the
    Resentful muttering Mass.

Whose ruminant hatred of all which cannot
Be simplified or stolen is still at large;
    No death can assuage its lust   105

To vilify the landscape of Distinction and see
The heart of the Personal brought to a systolic standstill,
　　The Tall to diminished dust.

Preserve me, Master, from its vague incitement;
Yours be the disciplinary image that holds   110
　　Me back from agreeable wrong
And the clutch of eddying muddle, lest Proportion shed
The alpine chill of her shrugging editorial shoulder
　　On my loose impromptu song.

Suggest; so may I segregate my disorder   115
Into districts of prospective value: approve;
　　Lightly, lightly, then, may I dance
Over the frontier of the obvious and fumble no more
In the old limp pocket of the minor exhibition,
　　Nor riot with irrelevance.   120

And no longer shoe geese or water stakes, but
Bolt in my day my grain of truth to the barn
　　Where tribulations may leap
With their long-lost brothers at last in the festival
Of which not one <u>had</u> [has] a dissenting image, and the   125
　　Flushed immediacy sleep.

Into this city from the shining lowlands
Blows a wind that whispers of uncovered skulls
　　And fresh ruins under the moon,
Of hopes that will not survive the secousse of this spring 130
Of blood and flames, of the terror that walks by night and
　　The sickness that strikes at noon.

All will be judged. Master of nuance and scruple,
Pray for me and for all writers living or dead;
　　Because there are many whose works   135
Are in better taste than their lives; because there is no end
To the vanity of our calling: make intercession
　　For the treason of all clerks.

Because the darkness is never so distant,
And there is never much time for the arrogant   140
    Spirit to flutter its wings,
Or the broken bone to rejoice, or the cruel to cry
For Him whose property is always to have mercy, the author
    And giver of all good things.

        The bracketed words above and additional stanzas below
        are from a version published in *Horizon*, III, 18 (1941).

Between stanzas 11 and 12:

Perhaps the honour of a great house, perhaps its
Cradles and tombs may persuade the bravado of
    The bachelor mind to doubt
The dishonest path, or save from disgraceful collapse
The creature's shrinking withness bellowed at and tickled
    By the huge Immodest Without.

Between stanzas 15 and 16:

Let this orchard point to its stable arrangement
Of accomplished bones as a proof that our lives
    Conceal a pattern which shows
A tendency to execute formative movements, to have
Definite experiences in their execution,
    To rejoice in knowing it grows.

Between stanzas 21 and 22:

Knowing myself a mobile animal descended
From an ancient line of respectable fish,
    With a certain méchant charm,
Occupying the earth for a grass-grown interval between
Two oscillations of polar ice, engaged in weaving
    His conscience upon its calm.

Despising Now yet afraid of Hereafter,
Unable in spite of his stop-watch and lens
    To imagine the rising Rome

To which his tools and tales migrate, to guess from what
      shore
The signal will flash, to observe the anarchists gestation
  In the smug constricted home.

A

At the Grave of Henry James

The snow, less intransigeant than their marble,
Has left the defence of whiteness to these tombs,
    And all the pools at my feet
Accommodate blue now, echo clouds as occur
To the sky, and whatever bird or mourner the passing   5
    Moment remarks they repeat.

While rocks, named after singular spaces
Within which images wandered once that caused
    All to tremble and offend,
Stand here in an innocent stillness, each marking the spot 10
Where one more series of errors lost its uniqueness
    And novelty came to an end.

To whose real advantage were such transactions,
When worlds of reflection were exchanged for trees?
    What living occasion can   15
Be just to the absent? Noon but reflects on itself,
And the small taciturn stone, that is the only witness
    To a great and talkative man,

Has no more judgement than my ignorant shadow
Of odious comparisons or distant clocks   20
    Which challenge and interfere
With the heart's instantaneous reading of time, time that is
A warm enigma no longer to you for whom I
    Surrender my private cheer,

As I stand awake on our solar fabric,   25
That primary machine, the earth, which gendarmes, banks
    And aspirin pre-suppose,
On which the clumsy and sad may all sit down, and any
        who will
Say their a-ha to the beautiful, the common locus
    Of the Master and the rose.   30

Shall I not especially bless you as, vexed with
My little inferior questions, I stand
    Above the bed where you rest,
Who opened such passionate arms to your Bon when It ran
Towards you with its overwhelming reasons pleading   35
    All beautifully in Its breast?

With what an innocence your hand submitted
To those formal rules that help a child to play,
    While your heart, fastidious as
A delicate nun, remained true to the rare noblesse   40
Of your lucid gift and, for its love, ignored the
    Resentful muttering Mass,

Whose ruminant hatred of all that cannot
Be simplified or stolen is yet at large:
    No death can assuage its lust   45
To vilify the landscape of Distinction and see
The heart of the Personal brought to a systolic standstill,
    The Tall to diminished dust.

Preserve me, Master, from its vague incitement;
Yours be the disciplinary image that holds   50
    Me back from agreeable wrong
And the clutch of eddying Muddle, lest Proportion shed
The alpine chill of her shrugging editorial shoulder
    On my loose impromptu song.

All will be judged. Master of nuance and scruple,   55
Pray for me and for all writers, living or dead:
    Because there are many whose works

Are in better taste than their lives, because there is no end
To the vanity of our calling, make intercession
   For the treason of all clerks.   60

1. An entirely different pattern of action is presented in the
A and B versions. By omitting stanzas that contain such direct
appeals as "O stern proconsul . . ." and so forth, and by waiting until stanza 9 of the final version for the affectionate
"Preserve me, Master . . ." the poet creates a tension or drama
not present in the earlier version. In what other ways has this
poem been reconstructed?
2. In stanza 7 of A, what emotion does the addition of the
"child" passage evoke?
3. Discuss the stanzas omitted from both the A and B versions. Do you think there is a connection between the two
major revisions?
4. In version B, do stanzas 7 and 8 offer anything significant to the development of theme?

B

To E. M. Forster

Here, though the bombs are real and dangerous,
And Italy and King's are far away,
And we're afraid that you will speak to us,
You promise still the inner life shall pay.

As we run down the slope of Hate with gladness   5
You trip us up like an unnoticed stone,
And just as we are closeted with Madness
You interrupt us like the telephone.

For we are Lucy, Turton, Philip, we
Wish international evil, are excited   10
To join the jolly ranks of the benighted

Where Reason is denied and Love ignored:
But, as we swear our lie, Miss Avery
Comes out into the garden with the sword.

Collected Poetry (1945)

A

Sonnets from China

(TO E. M. FORSTER)

Though Italy and King's are far away,
And Truth a subject only bombs discuss,
Our ears unfriendly, still you speak to us,
Insisting that the inner life can pay.

As we dash down the slope of hate with gladness,   5
You trip us up like an unnoticed stone,
And, just when we are closeted with madness,
You interrupt us like the telephone.

Yes, we are Lucy, Turton, Philip: we
Wish international evil, are excited   10
To join the jolly ranks of the benighted

Where reason is denied and love ignored,
But, as we swear our lie, Miss Avery
Comes out into the garden with a sword.

Collected Shorter Poems (1967)

1. Does one poem reveal the poet's attitude more clearly than the other? The most significant changes occur in the first quatrain. How do these early changes trigger the others? Or, do they not?

2. The nature of the bombs, or the poet's attitude towards them, has changed. What role has "Truth" in this context, and is the role extended throughout the poem?

3. There are a number of abstract personifications other than "Truth" creating an allegorical feeling, as though a universal drama were being acted out on stage. Our feelings towards these personifications are somewhat altered by the omission of capital letters. Discuss allegory and the use of these words in both versions.

4. The poem, in part at least, relies upon the reader's knowledge of certain works by E. M. Forster. The name "Lucy" and others are from Forster's novels. Is it legitimate for the poet to assume such knowledge on the part of his reader? How much may a poet take for granted?

B

Hongkong 1938

Its leading characters are wise and witty;
Substantial men of birth and education
With wide experience of administration,
They know the manners of a modern city.

Only the servants enter unexpected;   5
Their silence has a fresh dramatic use:
Here in the East the bankers have erected
A worthy temple to the Comic Muse.

Ten thousand miles from home and What's-her-name,
The bugle on the Late Victorian hill   10
Puts out the soldier's light; off-stage, a war

Thuds like the slamming of a distant door:
We cannot postulate a General Will;
For what we are, we have ourselves to blame.

    Collected Poetry (1945)

A

Hong Kong

Its leading characters are wise and witty,
Their suits well-tailored, and they wear them well,
Have many a polished parable to tell
About the mores of a trading city.

Only the servants enter unexpected,   5
Their silent movements make dramatic news;
Here in the East our bankers have erected
A worthy temple to the Comic Muse.

Ten thousand miles from home and What's-Her-Name
A bugle on this Late Victorian hill   10
Puts out the soldier's light; off-stage, a war

Thuds like the slamming of a distant door:
Each has his comic role in life to fill,
Though Life be neither comic nor a game.

Collected Shorter Poems (1967)

1. Though the picture of Hong Kong's "leading characters" is visually different in the two versions (that is, we see
different images), the tone and attitude are generally the
same. "Modern city" and "trading city" are very different
expressions, but Auden's context relates them connotatively.
Does the change in language between A and B in the first
stanza suggest a further shift in vision?
2. The change in the sixth line is of rhythm and prosody
as well as syntax. Note how the strong accents fall on "movements" and "news" in the A version. What effect does this
produce? Is the earlier version of the line smoother? Which
version makes better sense?
3. The last two lines are very different in each version.
Discuss the ways in which they are different and to what end.

✸

𝒜

In Memory of W. B. Yeats

(D. JAN. 1939)

I

He disappeared in the dead of winter:
The brooks were frozen, the airports almost deserted,
And snow disfigured the public statues;
The mercury sank in the mouth of the dying day.
What instruments we have agree [O all the instruments
           agree]   5
The day of his death was a dark cold day.

Far from his illness
The wolves ran on through the evergreen forests,
The peasant river was untempted by the fashionable quays;
By mourning tongues   10
The death of the poet was kept from his poems.

But for him it was his last afternoon as himself,
An afternoon of nurses and rumours;
The provinces of his body revolted,
The squares of his mind were empty,   15
Silence invaded the suburbs,
The current of his feeling failed; he became his admirers.

Now he is scattered among a hundred cities
And wholly given over to unfamiliar affections,
To find his happiness in another kind of wood   20
And be punished under a foreign code of conscience.
The words of a dead man
Are modified in the guts of the living.

But in the importance and noise of to-morrow
When the brokers are roaring like beasts on the floor of
        the Bourse,   25

And the poor have the sufferings to which they are fairly
    accustomed,
And each in the cell of himself is almost convinced of his
    freedom,
A few thousand will think of this day
As one thinks of a day when one did something slightly
    unusual.
<u>What instruments we have agree</u> [O all the instruments
    agree]   30
The day of his death was a dark cold day.

II

You were silly like us; your gift survived it all;
The parish of rich women, physical decay,
Yourself. Mad Ireland hurt you into poetry.
Now Ireland has her madness and her weather still,   35
For poetry makes nothing happen: it survives
In the valley of its <u>making</u> [saying] where executives
Would never want to tamper, <u>flows on</u> [it flows] south
From ranches of isolation and the busy griefs,
Raw towns that we believe and die in; <u>it survives,</u>   40
<u>A way of happening, a mouth.</u>

what's the difference?

III

Earth, receive an honoured guest:
William Yeats is laid to rest.
Let the Irish vessel lie
Emptied of its poetry.   45

In the nightmare of the dark
All the dogs of Europe bark,
And the living nations wait,
Each sequestered in its hate;

Intellectual disgrace   50
Stares from every human face,
And the seas of pity lie
Locked and frozen in each eye.

Follow, poet, follow right
To the bottom of the night,   55
With your unconstraining voice
Still persuade us to rejoice;

With the farming of a verse
Making a vineyard of the curse,
Sing of human unsuccess   60
In a rapture of distress;

In the deserts of the heart
Let the healing fountain start,
In the prison of his days
Teach the free man how to praise.   65

> *Collected Shorter Poems* (1967). The bracketed words
> above and additional stanzas below are from a version
> published in *Collected Poetry* (1945).

Between stanzas 1 and 2 of section III:

Time that is intolerant
Of the brave and innocent,
And indifferent in a week
To a beautiful physique,

Worships language and forgives
Everyone by whom it lives;
Pardons cowardice, conceit,
Lays its honours at their feet.

Time that with this strange excuse   *meaning?*
Pardoned Kipling and his views,
And will pardon Paul Claudel,
Pardons him for writing well.

1. Part One of this most famous of modern elegies is non-
elegiac in tone. Nowhere does the poet communicate remorse-
fulness over the death of W. B. Yeats. That is, the implicit
sympathy is immediately understated and general. The only

change in the text of the first part is one appropriate to the mood of uncommitted pessimism. Only in the light of such a contrived mood could line 26 be understood. There is a fairly realistic basis here. Indeed, only "a few thousand" at most would be personally moved by the death of the great poet— nature is not moved.

2. It is clear that the idea "poetry makes nothing happen" is the central motivation or impetus to Auden's handling of this occasional poem. How is this idea developed and finally modified or qualified by the end of the poem?

3. In Part Three a new rhythm, one most often encountered in light verse or jingles, enters the elegy. Blake too employs a musical tone in "The Tyger." How can we account for this movement at this stage in the action?

4. Following line 54 Auden develops the final affirmation —it is an affirmation not only of Yeats' poetic activity or poetry itself, but also of the human condition generally.

5. The omitted stanzas may be somewhat didactic in the announcement that "time . . . worships language"; however, anthologies continue to print the poem with these three stanzas. Can you provide a defense on either or both sides?

Dylan Thomas

1914—1953

DYLAN THOMAS was born in Swansea, Wales, and thirty-nine years later died in a hospital in New York. The quiet countryside of his early youth, rich in folk tradition and simple faith, illuminates our enduring picture of Thomas the lyricist, the poet of wonder and childhood. Urban America, however, with its "terminal hospitals," in both the literal and metaphorical sense, fills out the picture of an irascible poet who was somehow doomed.

Thomas is one of the most popular of modern English poets, especially among young readers. *Child's Christmas in Wales* and *Under Milkwood*, two long dramatic poems, have a following far out of proportion to the accessibility of his total work. Thomas is not a simple poet. He does not speak directly to a large audience, and yet it is a large audience indeed that responds to his poetry. There is little mystery in all this. Much of Thomas' fame rests upon his reputedly wild and bawdy personality, and his early death and a clearly self-destructive life style add to or satisfy the romantic imagination. This, and the more important fact that his poetry, both early and late, communicates an exuberant energy with which young readers can identify, suggest reasons to embrace the poetry of Dylan Thomas.

Unlike much romantic poetry, Thomas' is never vague. He writes often of his childhood and his style is intensely lyrical, but his images, even when obscure, are sharp and specific. Frequently the poetry is quite intellectual in the special way it makes demands on our ability to unravel or reorder complicated patterns of experience. He is rarely intellectual or philosophical in the sense of imposing an already oriented system of thought on a wide range of human experience.

The study of Thomas' poetry in this chapter should separate the popular image of Thomas, the wild, drunken Welshman, or the poet of fine sentiment, from the poet whose work is carefully wrought and finely conceived, though it is often resonant with moods of defiance and celebration. His poetry is, at times, associated with the early-nineteenth-century romantic style, but his is frequently more like the elaborate poetry of the seventeenth century, with exaggerated metaphor and paradox. We will read oddly connected imagery that lends a surrealistic element to his work. Yet there is an intensity and sureness of direction to his art that separates him from the surrealists. Too, his attitude toward his art is of a different order from those poets or any modernistic school for that matter.

We will also note that Thomas is a master of sound. He himself said that "poetry is sound," and often our appreciation of the wonderful sound patterns makes the sometimes private meanings easier to accept, or less bothersome. Though the materials of Thomas' poetry are public—for example, the Bible, images out of Freud, actual recorded events—there is always a private sense considering these materials. This private sense creates, at times, privacy rather than indirect communication, but as one critic has observed, that special or private vision, impossible to translate out of the poetry, is, in itself, something communicated.

The poems here reprinted are from *Collected Poems* (1952), and the earlier drafts are from Ralph Maud's 1966 edition of Dylan Thomas' *Notebooks*. This last volume is made up of four manuscript exercise books that Thomas kept between 1930 and 1934, years that were critical in the development of his poetry, from ages 15 to 19, and reflect the themes and currents that would make up the mature poetry. Thomas regarded these notebook drafts as drafts only and would use them years later to make fresh poems. Many of them, however, can be read as separate poems of a youthful period. After 1941 the poet stopped working from them.

Constantine Fitzgibbon, in his definitive biography, *The Life of Dylan Thomas* (1965), comments on the poet's style during the four-year period of the *Notebooks*, in which the work ". . . shows a progression towards a greater density of meaning as he twisted syntax, piled image upon image and juxtaposed unexpected adjectival nouns in his determination to produce maximum effects and the greater measure of poetic truth."

This was also a period of experimentation, and thus the reader will note a variety of lyric forms in the chapter as he will also grapple with obscurities that resulted from early experimentation.

The interested student can discover influences on Thomas, in a less digested form than in the final poems or in later poems. Furthermore, these drafts reveal how early materials, sometimes raw and very different from final products of experience, depend on first inspirations for first construction, though the final construction, form, and inspiration communicated may be very different from the early works.

There is a definite movement in the body of these poems, Fitzgibbons continues, from a "confessional and hortatory free verse . . . to a more regular, packed stanza. . . ." The unglossed image abounds, and readers of the poetry written after 1941 will notice that those poems are clearer as they are shorter. Such a late poem as "In My Craft or Sullen Art" reveals not only the concerns of these earlier drafts and finished poems but also a technique, a love for words, a sense of music that is always clear and inspiriting no matter the darknesses.

Collected Poems is not arranged chronologically. This chapter, therefore, varies from the general procedure of the book and follows, instead, Thomas' own ordering. Thus, the A versions are not dated, but are printed as they appear in the *Collected Poems*. The B versions are notated with date of composition and number as found in the *Notebooks*. Also, because of Thomas' extensive practice of reworking his drafts, we have varied from the established system of the book in another way. There is no indication in the *Notebooks* which word or words the poet preferred. Therefore, unlike in the preceding chapters, both words in brackets and words in footnotes represent variants.

B

The hunchback in the park,
A solitary mister
Propped between trees and water,

Going daft for fifty seven years,
Is [getting]¹ dafter,   5
A cripple children call at,
Half-laughing, by no other name than mister,
They shout hey mister
Running when he has heard them clearly
Past lake and rockery   10
On out of sight.

There is a thing he makes when quiet comes
To the young nurses with the children
And the three veteran swans,
Makes a thing inside the hanging head,   15
[A]² figure without fault
And sees it on the gravel paths
Or walking on the water.

The figure's frozen all the winter
Until the summer melts it down   20
To make a figure without fault.
[It is a poem and it is a woman figure.]

Mister, the children call, hey mister,
And the hunchback in the park
Sees the [wild/molten] figure on the water,
Misty, now mister,   25
[Calling 'Hey Mister']
Hears it's woman's voice;
Mister, it calls, hey mister,
And the hunchback smiles.

                         May 9, 1932

1930–1932 Notebook LVVV. NOTE: The apostrophe in
line 26 in the word "it's" is found in Thomas' notebook
version.

¹ going   ² creates a

A

The Hunchback in the Park

The hunchback in the park
A solitary mister
Propped between trees and water
From the opening of the garden lock
That lets the trees and water enter   5
Until the Sunday sombre bell at dark

Eating bread from a newspaper
Drinking water from the chained cup
That the children filled with gravel
In the fountain basin where sailed my ship   10
Slept at night in a dog kennel
But nobody chained him up.

Like the park birds he came early
Like the water he sat down
And Mister they called Hey mister   15
And truant boys from the town
Running when he had heard them clearly
On out of sound

Past lake and rockery
Laughing when he shook his paper
Hunchbacked in mockery   20
Through the loud zoo of the willow groves
Dodging the park keeper
With his stick that picked up leaves.

And the old dog sleeper
Alone between nurses and swans   25
While the boys among the willows
Made tigers jump out of their eyes
To roar on rockery stones
And the groves were blue with sailors

Made all day until bell time   30
A woman figure without fault
Straight as a young elm
Straight and tall from his crooked bones
That she might stand in the night
After the locks and chains   35

All night in the unmade park
After the railings and shrubberies
The birds the grass the trees the lake
And the wild boys innocent as strawberries
Had followed the hunchback   40
To his kennel in the dark.

1. Both poems communicate a certain sadness about life. The final version, however, with its added ambiguities, viz. line 4 and following, presents a richer development of the central emotion.

2. Discuss the various details of each version, namely line 7 of A and line 4 of B. How do these separate details or images constitute an attitude?

3. The "dog kennel" image is developed in A so that by the last stanza it becomes symbolic of grave. Is there any such development of image, metaphor, or symbol in the notebook draft?

4. Do you like the last line of B? Why? The A poem ends on an entirely different note. Compare the two endings in terms of the poem's eventual tone, rhythm, and general movement.

5. The hunchback dreams as do the children. His dream takes up a larger portion of the earlier draft than of the final version. Discuss the dream and its role in both versions.

B

After the funeral mule praises, brays,
Shaking of mule heads, betoken
Grief at the going to the earth of man
Or woman, at yet another long woe broken,
Another theme to play on and surprise   5
Fresh faults and till then hidden flaws
Faded beyond ears and eyes,
At [he or she],[1] loved or else hated well,
So far from love or hate, in a deep hole.

The mourners in their Sabbath black,   10
[Drop][2] tears unheeded or choke back a sob,
[Join][3] in the hymns, and mark with dry bright looks
The other [heads],[4] [bent],[5] [spying],[6] on black books.

Death has rewarded him or her for living,
With generous hands has slain with little pain,   15
[Wounded with a sharp sword,]
And let the ancient face die with a [smile].[7]

Another gossips' toy has lost its use
Broken lies buried and broken toys,
Of flesh and bone lies hungry for the flies,   20
Waits for the natron and the mummy paint,
With dead lips pursed and dry bright eyes,
Another well of rumours and cold lies
Has dried[, and one more [joke][8] has lost its point.]
                                February 10, 1933

        February, 1933, Notebook VI

    [1] him or her   [2] Dropped   [3] Joined   [4] masks   [5] spy   [6] mewling
[7] stain   [8] dart

A

After the Funeral

(IN MEMORY OF ANN JONES)

After the funeral, mule praises, brays,
Windshake of sailshaped ears muffle-toed tap
Tap happily of one peg in the thick
Grave's foot, blinds down the lids, the teeth in black,
The spittled eyes, the salt ponds in the sleeves,   5
Morning smack of the spade that wakes up sleep,
Shakes a desolate boy who slits his throat
In the dark of the coffin and sheds dry leaves,
That breaks one bone to light with a judgment clout,
After the feast of tear-stuffed time and thistles   10
In a room with a stuffed fox and a stale fern,
I stand, for this memorial's sake, alone
In the snivelling hours with dead, humped Ann
Whose hooded, fountain heart once fell in puddles
Round the parched worlds of Wales and drowned each sun 15
(Though this for her is a monstrous image blindly
Magnified out of praise; her death was a still drop;
She would not have me sinking in the holy
Flood of her heart's fame; she would lie dumb and deep
And need no druid of her broken body).   20
But I, Ann's bard on a raised hearth, call all
The seas to service that her wood-tongued virtue
Babble like a bellbuoy over the hymning heads,
Bow down the walls of the ferned and foxy woods
That her love sing and swing through a brown chapel,   25
Bless her bent spirit with four, crossing birds.
Her flesh was meek as milk, but this skyward statue
With the wild breast and blessed and giant skull
Is carved from her in a room with a wet window
In a fiercely mourning house in a crooked year.   30
I know her scrubbed and sour humble hands
Lie with religion in their cramp, her threadbare
Whisper in a damp world, her wits drilled hollow,
Her fist of a face died clenched on a round pain;

And sculptured Ann is seventy years of stone.   35
These cloud-sopped, marble hands, this monumental
Argument of the hewn voice, gesture and psalm,
Storm me forever over her grave until
The stuffed lung of the fox twitch and cry Love
And the strutting fern lay seeds on the black sill.   40

1. The notebook version is a more or less traditional elegy that generalizes upon and moves toward a moral about death. The sentiment is fairly standard: "betoken/Grief at the going to the earth . . ." and the images are expected rather than fresh: "the mourners in their Sabbath black/Drop tears . . ." The feeling of irony or cynicism underlying the elegiac rhythm hardly provides that richness which the final version finally does attain.

2. The final poem is an elegy on the death of Thomas' aunt, Ann Jones, and the reality of her life is contrasted throughout the poem with the unreality, or unnaturalness, of the funeral and the wake. Another contrast is that of the poet as one of the mourners and the poet as careful observer of these mourners.

3. The poem suggests a host of ideas concerning death, and ceremony, and the natural world. "The ferned and foxy woods" is set against the irrational or hypocritical earlier scene: "In a room with a stuffed fox and a stale fern."

4. The revised poem is more highly alliterative than the earlier draft. We are here feeling the influence of Anglo-Saxon or Welsh poetry or perhaps the alliterative verse of Hopkins. Alliteration is the repetition of initial identical consonant sounds or any vowel sounds in successive or closely associated words or syllables. The metrical structure in alliterative verse is based on periodic and regular repetition of certain initial letters or sounds within the lines. Discuss in line 31 alliteration, assonance, vowel pattern, and realism. How is this realism sustained, or current throughout the poem? And in line 34?

5. Toward what affirmation does the poem finally move?

C

The waking in a single bed when light
Fell on the upturned oval of her face
And morning's sun shone vast in the sky,
(Her last nights' lover), is gone forever,
Her [legal honour]¹ sold to one man for good   5
Who will disturb the [rhythms]² of her blood.
Where there was one are two, and nothing's shared
Of love and light in all this spinning world
Save the love-light of half love smeared
Over the countenance of the [two-backed]³ beast   10
Which nothing knows of rest but lust
And [lust],⁴ love knows, soon perishes the [breast],⁵
Reducing the [rose],⁶ for want of a [lovelier]⁷
Image on the ghost of paper,
Of single love to dust.   15

No longer with its touch kind as a mother's
Will the vibrations of [day]⁸ settle on
The pillow in [pale]⁹ lights where once she [lay alone],¹⁰
Heart [hardly beating]¹¹ under its [frame of ribs],¹²
Lips catching the honey of the golden   20
[Sun]¹³ small as a farthing
[Hiding]¹⁴ behind a cloud, for where
She lies another lies at her side,
And through his circling arm she feels
The secret coursing of his [undazzled] blood.   25
Filling her fingers with a hundred pins
Each sharper than the last.
And the [moon]¹⁵-ghost no longer
Will come as a stranger in the night
[Filling]¹⁶ her head with [moon's]¹⁷ light   30

Two lay where one lay lover for the sun.
Death, [last lover],¹⁸ is the lover to come.

---

¹ famous self   ² cellars   ³ bucking   ⁴ he   ⁵ ghost   ⁶ [ghost] midnight
sun   ⁷ wiser   ⁸ the sun   ⁹ wanting   ¹⁰ sank   ¹¹ all eyes and ears   ¹² roof
¹³ Ghost   ¹⁴ Hidden   ¹⁵ sun   ¹⁶ Crowding   ¹⁷ sun   ¹⁸ and his tongue,

Who, warm-veined, can love another
Mortal thing as an immortal lover?
No moon or sun, two taking one's couch,   35
Will shine the same, love each
As once he loved her who had one name.

It can be called a sacrifice. It can
With equal truth under the [vast sun][19]
Be [calling][20] the turning of sun'[21] love to man,
And now in the [cold night] [22]
There can be no warming by [sun's light].[23]

March 22, 1933

February, 1933, Notebook XVI

[19] just   [20] called   [21] s   [22] close   [23] sunlight

B

For a Woman Just Married

[ON THE MARRIAGE OF A]

The waking in a single bed when light
Struck [luckily her [skyscraping][1] face][2]
And morning's sun [rode][3] [hard][4] out of her thighs
(The last possessor), is gone forever,
Her moonstruck self [razed][5] for one guest for good.   5
Who will disturb the cellars of her blood.
Where there was one are two and nothing's shared
Of love and light in all [the hot],[6] the sunless world
[But][7] that [blind shadow][8] smeared
Over the countenance of the bucking beast,   10
And he, love knows, soon perishes the [ghost],[9]

[1] [mute] mazed [2] luckily the palaces of her face [3] trod [4] [proud]
[like a sun] true in the sky [5] sold [6] whole holy [7] Save [8] love-light
of half love [9] breast

Reducing the midnight sun, for want of a wiser
Image of the ghost of paper,
Of single love to dust.

No longer   15
Will the vibrations of the sun desire on
Her deepsea pillow where once she sank alone,
Her heart all ears and eyes, under
Lips catching the [avalanche][10] of the golden
Ghost small as a farthing   20
Hidden behind a cloud, for where
She lies [another][11] [lies][12] secret at her side,
And through his circling arm she feels
The [silent][13] coursing of his undazzled blood.

It can be called a sacrifice. It can   25
With equal truth under the [moon][14]
Be called the turning of sun's love to man,
And now in the [double][15] night
There can be no wild warming by [sun][16] light.

                              Revised January, 1941

[10] honey   [11] another's   [12] is   [13] secret   [14] [fled]
deserted sun   [15] closed   [16] sun's

A

On the Marriage of a Virgin

Waking alone in a multitude of loves when morning's light
Surprised in the opening of her nightlong eyes
His golden yesterday asleep upon the iris
And this day's sun leapt up the sky out of her thighs
Was miraculous virginity old as loaves and fishes,   5
Though the moment of a miracle is unending lightning
And the shipyards of Galilee's footprints hide a navy of doves.

No longer will the vibrations of the sun desire on
Her deepsea pillow where once she married alone,
Her heart all ears and eyes, lips catching the avalanche   10
Of the golden ghost who ringed with his streams her mercury
       bone,
Who under the lids of her windows hoisted his golden luggage,
For a man sleeps where fire leapt down and she learns through
       his arm
That other sun, the jealous coursing of the unrivalled blood.

1. Again, the final poem bears little resemblance to the
first draft(s). Besides a similarity in theme can you detect the
one image or metaphor from the B version that is developed
and transformed in the final poem?

2. Intrinsic to the sonnet form is a poem of fourteen lines,
the last two of which present a conclusion. Thomas, however,
wrote a number of irregular sonnets making frequent use of
assonance instead of rhyme or odd rhyming patterns, neither
of which is typical of the sonnet. Can you comment further
on the structural composition of this poem?

3. Who is the subject of the first five lines of the final
poem? How is she related to the virgin of stanza 2?

4. The image in line C2 is of the "upturned oval of her
face." This is a most concrete image; there is nothing abstract
in the conception. This image gives way to "Skyscraping/
mute/mazed face," and then, in the same B draft, to "palaces
of her face." In what direction is the poet heading with these
changes? In the final version Thomas uses "in the opening
of her nightlong eyes." Compare "nightlong" with "upturned
oval."

5. A collection of rather extravagant conceits has preceded
line 13, which is finally realistic. We can perceive a real lady
lying with a real man. Is Thomas merely jesting with his
wonderful sense of paradox (for example, lines 6, 9, and 11)
or are these jests or plays of wit essential to the final vision?

✵

C

The tombstone tells how she died.
She [wed]¹ on [a wild March]² morning;
Before she lay on her wedding bed
She died, was death's bride.
The tombstone tells how she died.   5
She [wed]³ on a [wild March morning],⁴
With March flowers over her head,
A farmer up valley who needed a [lass]⁵
To sleep with and talk with and [clean the pig sheds].⁶
She died in her white wedding dress,   10
With a garland of roses, a [Catholic cross],⁷
A cake, and a ring, and a [clean inside].⁸
[Her legs that showed death coming in.]
The tombstone tells how she died.

July, 1933

February, 1933, Notebook XXXVI

¹ married   ² some old Welsh   ³ married   ⁴ mad Welsh   ⁵ clean girl
⁶ milk and clean   ⁷ gold-eyed   ⁸ mirror inside

B

Poem

The tombstone told when she died.
Her two surnames stopped me still.
A virgin married at rest.
She married in this [raining]¹ place,
That I struck one day by luck,   5
Before I heard in my mother's side
Or saw in the looking-glass shell
The rain through her cold heart speak
And the sun killed in her face.
More the thick stone cannot tell.   10

¹ pouring

Before she lay on a [stranger's]² bed
With a hand plunged through her hair,
Or that [raining]³ tongue beat back
Through the [devilish]⁴ years and [innocent]⁵ *deaths*
To the room of a [secret]⁶ child,   15
Among men later I heard it said
She cried her white-dressed limbs were bare
And her red lips were kissed black,
She wept in her pain and made *mouths*,
Talked and tore though her eyes smiled.   20

I who saw in a [hurried]⁷ film
Death and this mad *heroine*
Met once on a mortal wall,
Heard her speak through the chipped beak
Of the [stone]⁸ bird guarding her: 25
I died before bedtime came
But my womb was *bellowing*
And I felt with my bare fall
A [blazing]⁹ red harsh head tear up
And the [dear]¹⁰ floods of his hair.   30

September, 1938, Laugharne

² farmer's   ³ small wet   ⁴ small   ⁵ great   ⁶ quiet   ⁷ winding
⁸ angel   ⁹ strange and   ¹⁰ great

A

The Tombstone Told When She Died

The tombstone told when she died.
Her two surnames stopped me still.
A virgin married at rest,
She married in this pouring place,
That I struck one day by luck,   5
Before I heard in my mother's side
Or saw in the looking-glass shell
The rain through her cold heart speak

And the sun killed in her face.
More the thick stone cannot tell.   10
Before she lay on a stranger's bed
With a hand plunged through her hair,
Or that rainy tongue beat back
Through the devilish years and innocent deaths
To the room of a secret child,   15
Among men later I heard it said
She cried her white-dressed limbs were bare
And her red lips were kissed black,
She wept in her pain and made mouths,
Talked and tore though her eyes smiled.   20
I who saw in a hurried film
Death and this mad heroine
Meet once on a mortal wall
Heard her speak through the chipped beak
Of the stone bird guarding her: 25
I died before bedtime came
But my womb was bellowing
And I felt with my bare fall
A blazing red harsh head tear up
And the dear floods of his hair.   30

1. The early version emphasizes a story. How does this emphasis shift in B and A?

2. The C version tells us of the lady's former husband. He is virtually absent in the final poem. Discuss the shift in point of view between the 1933 version and the final version.

3. The language is direct and clear in the final version—note line 10. There are lines in the notebook version C that foretell such clarity. In a sense, line C10 is simpler, more matter of fact. Comment on the difference in clarity.

4. Comment on the pattern of end-stopped and run-on lines. Thomas is using "sprung rhythm" in this poem. Gerard Manley Hopkins coined the term to designate the meter of poetry whose rhythm is based on the number of stressed syllables in a verse without regard to the number of unstressed syllables. The verses will be composed of combina-

tions of varying feet creating extreme rhetorical irregularity.
We will hear such rhythms again in a poem by Hopkins.

5. Note the eroticism of line A12. Is there a hint of this
development in the C version?

6. The B version contains a number of italicized words.
How are these words emphasized in the final version? Study
the poem's syntax and rhythm.

B

And death shall have no dominion.
Man, with soul naked, shall be one
With the man in the wind and the west moon,
With the harmonious thunder of the sun;
When his bones are picked clean and the clean bones gone,   5
He shall have stars at elbow and foot;
Though he fall mad he shall be sane,
And though he drown he shall rise up again;
Though lovers be lost love shall not;
Though he lose he shall gain;   10
And death shall have no dominion.

And death shall have no dominion.
Under green shiftings of the sea
Man shall [lie][1] long but shall not die,
And under the white darkness of the snow;   15
Twisting on racks when sinews give way,
Strapped to a wheel, yet he shall not break;
Faith in his hands shall snap in two,
And all the swords of evil run him through;
Split all ends up, he shan't crack;   20
And death shall have no dominion.

[1] belaid

Romans 6:9
*calling forth of
the dead at
the 2nd
coming —
end of
death*

*here the dominion over death
is achieved by man's
being made one with
nature.*

And death shall have no dominion.
No more may gulls cry at his ear,
Or waves break loud on the sea shore,
Telling some wonder to the salty air;   25
Where blew a flower may a flower no more
Lift its head to the blows of the rain;
Beauty may vanish at his stare,
And, when he shield his eyes, again be fair;
Beauty may blossom in pain;   30
And death shall have no dominion.

And death shall have no dominion.
Under the sea or snow at last
Man shall discover all he thought lost,
And hold his little soul within his fist;   35
Knowing that now can he never be dust,
He waits in the sun till the sun goes out;
Now he knows what he had but guessed
Of living and dying and all the rest;
He knows his soul. There is no doubt.   40
And death shall have no dominion.

April, 1933

February, 1933, Notebook XXIII

A

And Death Shall Have No Dominion

And death shall have no dominion.
Dead men naked they shall be one
With the man in the wind and the west moon;
When their bones are picked clean and the clean bones gone,
They shall have stars at elbow and foot;   5
Though they go mad they shall be sane,
Though they sink through the sea they shall rise again;
Though lovers be lost love shall not;
And death shall have no dominion.

And death shall have no dominion.   *green shiftings*   10
Under the windings of the sea
They lying long shall not die windily;
Twisting on racks when sinews give way,
Strapped to a wheel, yet they shall not break;
Faith in their hands shall snap in two,   15
And the unicorn evils run them through;   *swords of evil*
Split all ends up they shan't crack;
And death shall have no dominion.

And death shall have no dominion.
No more gulls cry at their ears   20
Or waves break loud on the seashores;
Where blew a flower may a flower no more
Lift its head to the blows of the rain;
Though they be mad and dead as nails,
Heads of the characters hammer through daisies;   25
Break in the sun till the sun breaks down,
And death shall have no dominion.

1. Discuss the poem's lyric quality, its rhythm, and its use of "symphonic vowels." The poem has an oratorical resonance. Does the change in pronouns in stanza 1 of A and B lend to this oratorical and public chanting effect? What other reasons do you see for the changes in the first stanza?

2. The B version is much longer than the final poem. What does the longer poem contain in terms of the poem's experience and in terms of its structure?

3. The poem is clearly about resurrection and certain values that transcend life. How do the minor changes affect our understanding of these themes? Comment on the minor changes.

C

Pass through twelve stages, reach the fifth
By retrograde moving from near death,
And puberty recoils at callow youth
Knowing such stuff as will confuse
That phantom in the blood, used to misuse,   5
Red rims, a little learning, and calf sense.
In carpet slippers, with a broken crutch,
Retrogress from pitch to pitch,
Leave the oncoming shadow at the door,
Leave it your odd shoes.   10
Let the scales fall from rheumy eyes,
And, stepping back through the medium of abuse,
Excess or otherwise, regain your fire.
Graft a monkey gland, old man, at fools' advice.

Shall it be male or female? say the cells,   15
The womb deliberates, spits forth manchild
To break or to be broken by the world,
A body cursed already by heredity.
The hundred-tainted lies in the cold and cools.

A one legged man ascending steps   20
Looks down upon him with regrets
That whips and stools and cistern sex
Have yet to add to that that mother strips
Upon her knee and shields from metal whisper
Of wind along the cot,   25
Sees cool get cold and childmind darker
As time on time sea ribbon rounds
Parched shires in dry lands.

The hundred-tainted must pulse and grow,
Victims of sires' vices breed heirs   30
To herring smelling fevers,
By way of ditch and gap arrive full stop.

Old man, would you arrive at pain,
Although new pain, by back lane,

Not dodging ruts but stepping through them,   35
Soaking old legs and veins,
And reach your youth again by them.

The child on lap is a nice child,
Has learnt, through cold, to love the heat,
On female knees takes a warm seat,   40
And this is all there is to it:
The victim of grandfather's
Unwise desires, or even earlier's,
Has a hundred stigmas,
More chance to hand on   45
Un clean Round Robin,
And more to hear air engine,
May yet find wings as airman,
And parachute old scabs and branded spots.

                              April 23, 1933

        February, 1933, Notebook XXVII

B

If I was tickled by the rub of love,
A rooking girl who stole me for her side,
Broke through her straws, breaking my bandaged string,
If the red tickle as the cattle calve
Still set to scratch a laughter from my lung,   5
I would not fear the apple nor its flood
Nor the bad blood of spring.

Shall it be male or female? says the cells,
And drop the plum like fire from the flesh.
If I was tickled by the hatching hair,   10
The winging bone that sprouted in the heels,
The itch of man upon the baby's thigh,
I would not fear the gallows nor the axe
Nor the crossed sticks of war.

[If from the first some mother of the wind   15
Gave suck to such a bud as forks my eye,
I would not fear the howling round the cots
As time on time the lean searibbons round
Parched shires in dry lands, and the rat's lot,
Nor all the herring smelling of the sea   20
Nor the death in the light.]

Shall it be male or female? say the fingers
Chalking the [jakes]¹ with green [things of]² [the brain]³
I would not fear the muscling-in of love
If I was tickled by the urchin hungers   25
Rehearsing heat upon a raw-edged nerve.
I would not fear the devil in the loin
Nor the outspoken grave.

If I was tickled by the lover's rub
That wipes away not crow's-foot nor the lock   30
Of sick old [age]⁴ up on the falling jaws:
Time and the crabs and the sweethearting crib
Would leave me cold as butter for the flies:
[The biting days would soften as I struck
Bells on the dead fools']⁵ toes.   35

This world is half the devil's and my own,
Daft with the drug that's smoking in a girl
And curling round the bud that forks her eye.
An old man's shank one-marrowed with my bone,
And all the herrings smelling in the sea,   40
I sit and watch the worm beneath my nail
Wearing the quick away.

And that's the rub, the only rub that tickles.
The knobbly ape that swings along his sex
From damp love-darkness and the nurse's twist   45
Can never raise the midnight of a chuckle,

---

¹ walls   ² girls   ³ their men   ⁴ manhood   ⁵ The sea of scums could
drown me as it broke/Dead on the sweethearts

Nor when he finds a beauty in the breast
Of lover, mother, lovers or his six
Feet in the rubbing dust.

And what's the rub? Death's feather on the nerve?   50
Your mouth, my love, the thistle in a kiss?
My Jack of Christ born thorny on the tree?
The words of death are dryer than his stiff,
My wordy wounds are printed with your hair.
I would be tickled by the rub that is: 55
Man be my metaphor.

      April 30, 1934

      August, 1933, Notebook XLI

A

If I Were Tickled by the Rub of Love

If I were tickled by the rub of love,
A rooking girl who stole me for her side,
Broke through her straws, breaking my bandaged string,
If the red tickle as the cattle calve
Still set to scratch a laughter from my lung,   5
I would not fear the apple or the flood
Nor the bad blood of spring.

Shall it be male or female? say the cells,
And drop the plum like fire from the flesh.
If I were tickled by the hatching hair,   10
The winging bone that sprouted in the heels,
The itch of man upon the baby's thigh,
I would not fear the gallows nor the axe
Nor the crossed sticks of war.

Shall it be male or female? say the fingers   15
That chalk the walls with green girls and their men.
I would not fear the muscling-in of love

If I were tickled by the urchin hungers
Rehearsing heat upon a raw-edged nerve.
I would not fear the devil in the loin   20
Nor the outspoken grave.

If I were tickled by the lovers' rub
That wipes away not crow's-foot nor the lock
Of sick old manhood on the fallen jaws,
Time and the crabs and the sweethearting crib   25
Would leave me cold as butter for the flies,
The sea of scums could drown me as it broke
Dead on the sweetheart's toes.

This world is half the devil's and my own,
Daft with the drug that's smoking in a girl   30
And curling round the bud that forks her eye.
An old man's shank one-marrowed with my bone,
And all the herrings smelling in the sea,
I sit and watch the worm beneath my nail
Wearing the quick away.   35

And that's the rub, the only rub that tickles.
The knobbly ape that swings along his sex
From damp love-darkness and the nurse's twist
Can never raise the midnight of a chuckle,
Nor when he finds a beauty in the breast   40
Of lover, mother, lovers, or his six
Feet in the rubbing dust.

And what's the rub? Death's feather on the nerve?
Your mouth, my love, the thistle in the kiss?
My Jack of Christ born thorny on the tree?   45
The words of death are dryer than his stiff,
My wordy wounds are printed with your hair.
I would be tickled by the rub that is:
Man be my metaphor.

  1. The B version is very much like the final poem except
for a few minor changes, which make the final poem more

precise. The third stanza in B is excluded. What are your thoughts on this stanza? Does it contain ideas present already in the poem? Does it change anything other than the poem's structure?

2. The poem develops around a series of fears or anxieties. Does C, a poem vastly different from the other versions, clarify this thematic development in any way? The C poem contains lines that eventually are found in the final poem. Cite these lines and discuss their function in the two poems.

3. Discuss the early version and the finished poem from the point of view of dramatic design or structure.

4. Discuss literary allusions in poetry generally and in this poem specifically, for example, "Aye, there's the rub" from *Hamlet*.

B

Especially when the November wind
With frosty fingers punishes my hair,
Or, beaten on by the straight beams of the sun,
I walk abroad, feeling my youth like fire
Burning weak blood and body up,   5
Does the brain reel, drunk on the raw
Spirits of words, and the heart sicken
Of arid syllables grouped and regrouped with care,
Of the chosen task that lies upon
My belly like a cold stone.   10

By the sea's side hearing the cries of gulls,
In winter fields hearing a sheep cough
That wakes out of tubercular oblivion
Into a wet world, my heart rebells
Against the chain of words,   15
Now hard as iron and now soft as clouds,
While weighted trees lift asking arms far off.

Shut in a tower of words, I mark
Men in the distance walk like trees
And talking as the four winds talk,   20
Children in parks and children's homes
Speaking on fingers and thumbs,
And think, as drummed on by the sun,
How good it is to feel the November air
And be no words' prisoner.   25

To view the changing world behind
A pot of ferns, lifting the sunblind
See gilded people walking on hindlegs
Along the pavement where a blind man begs
Hopefully, helplessly, feeling the sun's wings,   30
To trim a window garden with a shears,
To read front pages, fall asleep,
Undreaming, on a linen lap
This, when the heart goes sick
And ears are threatened in the spring of dawn   35
By the triumphant accents of the cock,
Is more to be longed for in the end
Than, chained by syllables at hand and foot,
Wagging a wild tongue at the clock,
Deploring death, and raising roofs   40
Of words to keep unharmed
By time's approach in a fell wind
The bits and pieces of dissected loves.

A

Especially When the October Wind

Especially when the October wind
With frosty fingers punishes my hair,
Caught by the crabbing sun I walk on fire
And cast a shadow crab upon the land,
By the sea's side, hearing the noise of birds,   5

Hearing the raven cough in winter sticks,
My busy heart who shudders as she talks
Sheds the syllabic blood and drains her words.

Shut, too, in a tower of words, I mark
On the horizon walking like the trees   10
The wordy shapes of women, and the rows
Of the star-gestured children in the park.
Some let me make you of the vowelled beeches,
Some of the oaken voices, from the roots
Of many a thorny shire tell you notes,   15
Some let me make you of the water's speeches.

Behind a pot of ferns the wagging clock
Tells me the hour's word, the neural meaning
Flies on the shafted desk, declaims the morning
And tells the windy weather in the cock.   20
Some let me make you of the meadow's signs;
The signal grass that tells me all I know
Breaks with the wormy winter through the eye.
Some let me tell you of the raven's sins.

Especially when the October wind   25
(Some let me make you of autumnal spells,
The spider-tongued, and the loud hill of Wales)
With fists of turnips punishes the land,
Some let me make you of the heartless words.
The heart is drained that, spelling in the scurry   30
Of chemic blood, warned of the coming fury.
By the sea's side hear the dark-vowelled birds.

1. It is necessary to read this poem aloud. Where in the poem does Thomas tell us this?

2. This poem, as are a number of Thomas', is about the writing (or "making" or "telling") of poetry. The second stanza conveys a paradox of the imprisonment of the poet in his craft and his freedom to transform physical reality. In the earlier draft the stanza has an optimistic last line not

in the final poem. How does the line strike you in light of the entire poem?

3. The romantic tone in lines 4 and 5 of version B are nowhere to be found, or felt, in the final version. Thomas has "made" his poem not only structurally tighter, but also more objectified in terms of the expression of his personal experience. At the same time, however, consider the change from "November" in B to "October" in A, the month of the poet's birth. Discuss the images in lines 9 and 10 of B. Although the imagery is clear, and also dramatic, Thomas obviously had second thoughts about using it. How is it at variance with the final development of imagery?

4. Comment on the change of gender in stanza 2.

5. Line 26 of B begins a narrative movement not to be felt at all in A. Are any of the materials or tones of this narrative finally transformed in the later poem?

6. The last stanza recalls the first through a number of poetic devices, for example, rhymes and repetition of words, phrases, and images. What does Thomas accomplish through this conscious echoing? Does the earlier version have a similar design?

C

This minute's locked to learn me in the hour,
Who sees it burn to break the scriptured cell
And play the truant on the tip of days?
I, [rang]¹ the locks at my temple, but
But [burn and break]² no [marked]³ boy, or beast, or taper
First vision that set fire to the air
In a [room]⁴ [with]⁵ the [town].⁶

---

¹ said ² sentinel the burn and break ³ cap ⁴ square room ⁵ above
⁶ final town

B

This minute's locked to learn me in the hour,
[Who][1] sees it burn to break the chiming cell
And play the truant in the den of days
[Chock][2] with my [written heart and slate-grey hair][3]
[Chock-loud][4] chimed the ground

[1] [O] And [2] Loud [3] [scribbling blood] fringed rod and talking script
[4] in the

A

The minute is a prisoner in the hour
Lest brain keep [watch][1] will break [its hours'][2] cell
And play the truant in the den of days;
But, [arrow-eyed],[3] my senses shall not lose,
Nor sentinel my heart set free the frail   5
First vision that set fire to the [air].[4]

A minute wound that wonderment about,
When on the stivy wind a giant's voice
Told truth and rang the valley with its crying;
With falling wind down fell the giant's shout,   10
The meaning dropped and truth fled to the grass.
Deep in the valley's herbs I hear it dying.

Some see a living vision of the truth,
And some hear truth upon the wind, once only.
Forget, it dies, and lose, it's never found.   15
I shall remember losing until death,
Keep in my memory the minute lonely
Of truth that told the deaf and showed the blind.

August, 1933

February, 1933, Notebook LI

[1] Now [2] the striking/chiming [3] Angus [4] years/stars

1. These drafts all represent attempts by Thomas to make a poem. However, the poem was never finalized. We may guess as to why the poet abandoned the poem.

2. Although the poet was never completely satisfied with the poem, the various drafts are worthy of study as language workings, rather than merely as preludes to a final poem.

3. What is the central idea motivating Thomas' manipulation of language?

B

TO E. P.

The force that through the green fuse drives the flower
Drives my green age; that blasts the roots of trees
Is my destroyer.
And I am dumb to tell the eaten rose
How at my sheet goes the same crooked worm,   5
And dumb to holla thunder to the skies
How at my cloth flies the same central storm.

The force that through the green fuse drives the flower
Drives my green age, that blasts the roots of trees
Is my destroyer.   10
And I am dumb to tell the crooked rose
My youth is bent by the same wintry fever.

The force that drives the water through the rocks
Drives my red blood; that dries the mouthing streams
Turns mine to wax.   15
And I am dumb to mouth unto my veins
How at the mountain spring the same mouth sucks.

The hand that whirls the water in the pool
Stirs the quicksand; that ropes the blowing wind
Hauls my shroud sail.   20

And I am dumb to tell the hanging man
How of my clay is made the hangman's lime.

The lips of time leech to the fountain head;
Love drips and gathers, but the fallen blood
Shall make her well;   25
And I am dumb to tell the aimless sun
[How time is all.]

And I am dumb to tell the lover's tomb
How at my sheet goes the same crooked worm.

October 12, 1933

August, 1933, Notebook XXIII

A

The Force That Through the Green Fuse Drives the Flower

The force that through the green fuse drives the flower
Drives my green age; that blasts the roots of trees
Is my destroyer.
And I am dumb to tell the crooked rose
My youth is bent by the same wintry fever.   5

The force that drives the water through the rocks
Drives my red blood; that dries the mouthing streams
Turns mine to wax.
And I am dumb to mouth unto my veins
How at the mountain spring the same mouth sucks.   10

The hand that whirls the water in the pool
Stirs the quicksand; that ropes the blowing wind
Hauls my shroud sail.
And I am dumb to tell the hanging man
How of my clay is made the hangman's lime.   15

The lips of time leech to the fountain head;
Love drips and gathers, but the fallen blood
Shall calm her sores.
And I am dumb to tell a weather's wind
How time has ticked a heaven round the stars.   20

And I am dumb to tell the lover's tomb
How at my sheet goes the same crooked worm.

1. This poem is about the poet's youth and the natural
forces working on his sensibility and physical sense of life.
Discuss the rhythm and various patternings of sound in relation to the poem's central theme or idea.

2. This is one of Thomas' simplest poems. Yet its vast suggestiveness and ambiguities provide the reader with endless
possibilities for interpretation. Where is the poem most true,
for example, where do ambiguities gather? Discuss the paradox of a clear, yet difficult image.

3. Discuss repetition—tonal and intellectual—in the poem,
and discuss how these echoes or repetitions are shifted in
order to carry various meanings.

4. Consider the image beginning at line 14 in the earlier
version. What effect does its omission have in the later poem?

5. The rhythm of the poem is rising and falling (there is a
short stop, a caesura, after each semicolon) as the central
theme involves opposite poles of life and death, fruition and
decay, mortality and immortality, and so on. Discuss this
rhythm by citing the difference in line length and stress on
individual words. Do the same with version B.

6. The poem ends with a two-line coda. The earlier version
provides this conclusion as the fourth and fifth lines of the
first stanza. How does a change affect the poem?

John Keats

1795—1821

Because of the intensity and brevity of their lives, as well as the style and content of their poetry, a number of English poets have been given by succeeding generations the title "Romantic." Romanticism, as a philosophical and literary movement, is generally associated with the rise and exaltation of individualism, radical political thought, creative freedom, and reaction against neoclassical dictates of objectivity, clarity, and imitation. These might be exemplified, particularly in poetry, by many qualities, for example, heightened sensibility, extravagant imagination, references to both the self and nature, use of old verse forms, and fascination with the remote or primitive. The poet, by definition, seemed to embody many of these characteristics.

John Keats is one of a number of English Romantic poets who died young. In the *Oxford History of English Literature*, Ian Jack quotes a fellow student of Keats: "Poetry was . . . the zenith of all his aspirations: the only thing worth the attention of superior minds: so he thought: all other pursuits were mean and tame. . . . The greatest men in the world were poets and to rank among them was the chief object of his ambition."

Before dedicating his life to poetry, Keats pursued a course directed toward medicine. In 1815, he was working in the London Hospital, but by September 1816, he had given up medicine for poetry.

His belief or developing philosophical attitude toward poetry is an elusive matter of which to speak. His letters are rich with references to poetry, but the terms he employs defy systematic definition. Keats says that through apprehension of the beautiful man is able to connect with "the highest reality" or "essences" of the physical universe. This in turn leads to man's deepest happiness. Truth is tied up with perception of the beautiful—"a truth of sensation." We are led to a philosophy of impression and feelings rather than a systematic ordering and analysis of empirical or spiritual knowledge. However, as the reader of Keats' great odes already knows, there is a depth of thought, a reflectiveness that transcends mere loveliness or sensation of feeling.

Keats' first volume of *Poems* appeared in 1817 to few and unenthusiastic reviews. The early poems already show a concentration on sensual imagery not always rooted in the real world. Although this might be termed "poetry of escape," for example, escape into Spenser's world of faerie, a land far from the mundane realm of medical studies, Keats is rarely fanciful. Even in his early poetry there is the mark of authenticity, a concern for life as it is now.

Endymion, an ambitious work of great length, appeared in 1818 and shows the influence of Shakespeare's style, diction, and imagery. While the poem does exhibit many of the excesses of Romantic effusiveness, a "soft lusciousness of style," here Keats was attempting to move toward what he regarded as the "impersonality of Shakespeare," or what Matthew Arnold about fifty years later would call "disinterestedness." Keats liked the way in which Shakespeare stepped back from and refused to enter the lives of his characters. In a short time Keats moved toward this objectivity in art. In *Endymion*, as in the poems to follow, the persistent influence of the English Renaissance is felt. *Endymion* was attacked by the critical press, and Keats was beginning to grow accustomed to the viciousness of critics.

Most of Keats' great poetry was written between September 1818 and September 1819. The product of this short period is *Lamia, Isabella, The Eve of St. Agnes and Other Poems* (1820), which has been called the greatest single volume of English poetry of the nineteenth century. Through this volume in particular, Keats became the greatest influence of his age on the following period in poetry, an influence epitomized by his effect on Robert Browning.

The Eve of St. Agnes is a tale of youthful, romantic love set against a background of family feud, revelry, tempest, and bitter cold. This poem, which many feel to be Keats' crowning achievement, is based on popular superstitions with echoes of Gothic Romances, Shakespeare's plays, and folk tales reverberating throughout its stanzas.

While the poem rests on the popular legend about St. Agnes' Eve, Keats went to Spenser, the most elaborate of Elizabethans, for his stanza, music, lavish adornment of narrative, sensuous imagery, and medieval matter. The Spenserian stanza has nine lines rhyming ababbcbcc; the first eight lines are iambic pentameter, the last line an Alexandrine, a verse line with six iambic feet. The stanza itself is most suited for this narrative; it is processional in its movement and offers opportunities for richer effects of vowel music and sensuous luxury. The use of color and architectural detail are embellishments, to be sure, but, too, these elements epitomize states of mind and emotional levels reached by the characters in the poem.

The Eve of St. Agnes is built on many antitheses that demonstrate an internal drama going on beyond the simple drama of the lovers. Patterns of warmth and cold, color and colorlessness, tumultuous sound and silence are continually interwoven.

The beauties of this poem are revealed by a close examination of its language rather than by the kind of structural analysis to which much modern poetry lends itself. For a close study of the poem we are indebted to M. R. Ridley's *Keats' Craftsmanship: A Study in Poetic Development* (New York: Russell & Russell, 1962). Ridley records the genesis of the poem from about January 18, 1819. He collates the four written copies of the poem with the final version printed in 1820. However, there remain a few editorial problems. Ridley himself admits that in scattered instances (namely stanzas 36 and 37) there is uncertainty as to the precise wording. Each editor has his own idea as to authenticity.

Unlike the preceding chapters, this one contains only one poem, *The Eve of St. Agnes*. Because it is a relatively long poem, and the number of alterations are many, the poem stands alone as a chapter. This chapter presents only an A version with the early variations and later deletions indicated in the poem. Here again, as in the Auden chapter, the bracketed words are earlier variants that were replaced in the final

version by the underlined words. However, a number of
stanzas went through extensive reworking, too numerous to
include all minor changes here. Therefore, where interesting
variants occur the commentary draws the reader's attention
to these changes. We see the material developing and also get
an inkling of how Keats' mind worked through these changes.

In this chapter the questions and commentary are num-
bered according to the stanza to which they refer.

The Eve of St. Agnes

1

St. Agnes' Eve—Ah, bitter chill [cold] it was!
The owl, for all his feathers, was a-cold;
The hare limped trembling through the frozen grass,
And silent was [were] the flock in woolly fold:
Numb were the Beadsman's fingers, while he told
His rosary, and while his frosted breath,
Like pious incense from [in] a censer old,
Seemed taking flight for heaven, without a death,
Past the sweet Virgin's picture, while his prayer he saith.

2

His prayer he saith, this patient, holy man;
Then takes his lamp, and riseth from his knees,
And back returneth, meagre, barefoot, wan,
Along the chapel aisle by slow degrees:
The sculptured dead, on each side, seem to freeze,
Emprisoned in black, purgatorial rails:
Knights, ladies, praying in dumb orat'ries,
He passeth by; and this weak spirit fails
To think how they may ache in icy hoods and mails.

3 a

But there are ears may hear sweet melodies,
And there are eyes to brighten festivals,
And there are feet for nimble minstrelsies,

And many a lip that for the red wine calls—
Follow, then follow to the illumin'd halls,
Follow me youth—and leave the Eremite—
Give him a tear—then trophied banneral
And many a brilliant tasseling of light
Shall droop from arched ways this high Baronial night.

3

Northward he turneth through a little door,
And scarce three steps, ere Music's golden tongue
Flattered to tears this aged man and poor;
But no—already had his deathbell rung:
The joys of all his life were said and sung:
His was harsh penance on St. Agnes' Eve:
Another way he <u>went</u>, [turn'd;] and soon among
<u>Rough</u> [Black] ashes sat he for his soul's reprieve,
And all night kept awake, for sinner's <u>sake</u> [souls] to grieve.

4

That ancient Beadsman heard the prelude soft;
And so it chanced, for many a door was wide,
From hurry to and fro. Soon, up—[and now] aloft,
The silver, snarling trumpets 'gan to chide:
<u>High-lamped</u> [The level] chambers, ready with their
    pride,
<u>Were glowing</u> [Seem'd anxious] to receive a thousand
    guests:
The carved angels, ever eager-eyed,
Stared, where upon their heads the cornice rests,
With hair blown back, and wings put cross-wise on their
    breasts.

STANZA 1: The changes in stanza 1 may have been typographical corrections on the type proofs. Do you see, as Keats obviously saw, the need to correct these few words in this stanza? Characterize these changes.

STANZA 3A: Stanza 4 introduces the reader to a festive scene, the place of the opening action. 3a makes this introduction more gradual and more elaborate. The omission of the stanza gets us into the action more swiftly and with less pretense of narrative accuracy. There is no need for a narrative poem to provide each step of the story. Often dramatic tension is created by omission of detail.

STANZA 3: The omission of "turn'd" in line 7 is interesting for it is clearly a more dramatic word than his preferred "went." What virtue has this gained simplicity in the context of the developing narrative? in the stanza itself? "Turn'd" would be an echo from the first line. Is such an echo unfortunate? What effect is lost? What is gained? Discuss similarly the change in the last line from "souls" to "sake."

STANZA 4: Comment on the changes in lines 3 and 5. Both changes heighten drama and texture, yet they work in very different ways.

The "chambers" in line 5 are ready to receive guests. Whether they "glow" or "seem anxious" depends upon the kind of personification the poet chooses. Which personification seems more reasonable? Many kinds of personification are used in poetry and the best is not always the most fanciful or extravagant. The entire question of poetic decorum is at issue here. Also, the two choices presented differ in that one presents an image, while the other is difficult to picture in the mind.

5a

At length burst [step] in the argent revelry, [revelers]
With plume, tiara, and all rich array,
Ah what are they? the idle pulse scarce stirs,
The muse should never make the spirit gay;
Away, bright dulness, laughing fools away,—
And let me tell of one sweet lady there
Whose heart had brooded, all that wintry day,
On love, and winged St. Agnes' saintly care,
As she had heard old dames [Dames] full many times declare.

5

At length burst in the argent revelry,
With plume, tiara, and all rich array,
Numerous as shadows haunting faerily
The brain, new stuffed, in youth, with triumphs gay
Of old romance. These let us wish away,
And turn, sole-thoughted, to one Lady there,
Whose heart had brooded, all that wintry day,
On love, and winged St. Agnes' saintly care,
As she had heard old dames full many times declare.

6a

'Twas said her future lord would there appear
Offering as sacrifice—all in the dream—
Delicious food even to her lips brought near:
Viands and wine and fruit and sugar'd cream,
To touch her palate with the fine extreme
Or relish: then soft music heard; and then
More pleasures followed in a dizzy stream
Palpable almost: then to wake again
Warm in the virgin morn, no weeping Magdalen.

6

They told her how, upon St. Agnes' Eve,
Young virgins might have visions of delight.
And soft adorings from [of] their loves receive
Upon the honeyed middle of the night,
If ceremonies due they did aright;
As, supperless to bed they must retire,
And couch [lay] supine their beauties, lily white;
Nor look behind, nor sideways, but require
Of Heaven with upward eyes for all that they desire.

7

Full of this whim was thoughtful Madeline:
The music, yearning like a God in pain,

[Touch'd not her heart] She scarcely heard: her maiden
    eyes divine,
Fixed on the floor, saw many a sweeping train
Pass by—she heeded not at all: in vain
Came many a tiptoe, amorous cavalier,
And back retired; not cooled by high disdain,
But she saw not: her heart was otherwhere:
She sighed for Agnes' dreams, the sweetest of the year.

8

She danced along with vague, regardless eyes, [uneager
    look]
Anxious her lips, her breathing quick and short:*
The hallowed hour was near at hand: she sighs [—and]
Amid the timbrels, [Timbrels] and the thronged resort
Of whisperers [Whisperers] in anger, or in sport;
'Mid looks of love, [Love] defiance, hate, and scorn,
Hoodwinked with faery [She was hoodwink'd with]
    fancy; all amort,
Save to St. Agnes and her lambs [Lambs] unshorn,
And all the bliss to be before tomorrow morn.

STANZA 5: This stanza has been entirely recast. Discuss the
changes, especially in lines 3–6 in terms of developing action,
rhyme scheme, and total effect.

STANZA 6: Here we have the ritual detail of the superstition
about St. Agnes' Eve told to us by the "old dames." In 6a
other details are provided, most likely from a literary source
other than that which provided the materials for 6. There is
information in the omitted stanza (6a) essential to the entire
structure of the poem. Questions are left in the reader's mind
regarding Madeline's words upon waking (stanza 35). Answers may be provided out of the material in 6a. It has been

---

* A variant for line 2 reads: "Her anxious mouth full pulpd with rosy
thoughts—"

suggested that the stanza was omitted because readers found it over "sensual." Do you find the sensuality at odds with the development of language and imagery thus far in the poem?

STANZA 8: From this stanza forward Ridley examines Keats' own first draft. Up to this point, we have been working from the second draft manuscript as the preceding stanzas were lost in first draft state. The corrections here do not represent any single method of composition, that is, Keats crossed out a phrase and immediately put in another, as the printed text here would lead one to suspect. Rather, ". . . by corrections and interlinear insertions he got them into a condition which a compositor would have set as the second version." Treat these changes in the same way you have been doing throughout the text.

Consider the changes in the first three lines. When does the suggestiveness in a phrase give way to mere vagueness?

9

So, purposing each moment to retire,
She lingered still [fearful who might]. Meantime, across
    the moors,
Had come young Porphyro, with heart on fire [afire]
For Madeline. Beside [Within] the portal doors, [Portal
    Doors]
Buttressed from moonlight, stands he, and implores
All saints to give him sight of Madeline,
But for one moment in the tedious hours,
That he might gaze and worship all unseen; [or speak,
    or kneel]
Perchance speak, kneel, touch, kiss—in sooth such things have
    been.

1 0

He ventures in: let no buzzed whisper tell:
All eyes be muffled, or a hundred swords

Will storm his heart, Love's fev'rous citadel:
For him, those chambers held barbarian hordes,
Hyena foemen, and hot-blooded lords,
Whose very dogs would execrations howl
Against his lineage: not one breast affords
Him any mercy, in that mansion foul,
Save one old beldame, weak in body and in soul.

1 1

Ah, happy chance, the agéd creature came,
[Tottering] Shuffling along with ivory-headed wand,
    [staff]
To where he stood, hid from the torch's flame,
Behind a broad [huge] hall-pillar, far beyond
The sound of merriment and chorus bland:
He startled her; but soon she knew his face,
And grasped his fingers in her palsied hand,
Saying, "Mercy, Porphyro! hie thee from this place:
They are all here tonight, the whole blood-thirsty race!

1 2

"Get hence! get hence! there's dwarfish Hildebrand;
He had a fever late, and in the fit
He curséd thee and thine, both house and land:
Then there's that old Lord Maurice, not a whit
More tame for his gray hairs—Alas me! flit!
Flit like a ghost away."—"Ah, Gossip dear,
We're safe enough; here in this arm-chair sit,
And tell me how"—"Good Saints [Gods]! not here, not
    here;
Follow me, child, [—hush hush] or else these stones will be
    thy bier."

STANZA 9: The action is moved along, after a feeling of stasis
in the three previous stanzas, by the entrance of Porphyro.
In an earlier version line 2 delayed the suspense even longer.

The deletion of "fearful who might" is evidence that Keats
desired the action to pick up. A different observation may be
made at line 4. Here Keats leaves Porphyro "Beside" rather
than "Within" the doors to justify the following line realistically. The changes here also determine the reader's response to the nature of the hero. For example, in an earlier
draft "piteous" preceded ". . . implore/All saints . . ."

STANZA 10: There were a number of changes in this stanza,
both dramatic and metaphysical. The first three lines read:

He ventures in wrapped in a dark disguise
Let no Man see him, or a hundred Swords
Will storm his heart for all his amorous sighs

Comment on the revised opening.

STANZA 12: In the two changes consider the muting of tone.
The hero is in danger. How is this handled and what effect
does such toning down have on the entire development here?

1 3

He followed through a lowly archéd way,
Brushing the cobwebs with his lofty plume,
And as she mutter'd "Well-a—well-a-day!"
He found him in a little moonlight room,
Pale, latticed, chill, [casemented] and silent as a tomb.
"Now tell me where is Madeline," said he,
"O tell me, Angela [Goody], by the holy loom
Which none but secret [holy] sisterhood may see,
When they St. Agnes' wool are weaving [do weave full]
      piously."

1 4

"St. Agnes! Ah! it is St. Agnes' Eve—
Yet men will murder upon holy days [holidays]:
Thou must hold water in a witch's sieve,
And be liege-lord of all the Elves and Fays,

To venture so: it fills me with [in truth it doth] amaze
[Young Signor] To see thee, Porphyro!—St. Agnes' Eve!
God's help! my lady fair the conjuror plays
This very night: good angels her deceive!
But let me laugh awhile, I've mickle time to grieve."

1 5

Feebly she laugheth [laughd] in the [bright] languid
    moon
While Porphyro upon her face doth look,
Like puzzled [As doth an] urchin on an aged crone
Who keepeth closed a wond'rous riddle-book.
As spectacled she sits in chimney nook.
But soon his eyes grew brilliant, when she told
His lady's purpose; and he scarce could brook
Tears, at the thought of those enchantments cold,
And Madeline asleep in lap of [among those] legends old.

1 6

Sudden a thought came like a full-blown rose,
Flushing his brow [Young Cheek], and in his painéd
    [painful] heart
Made purple riot: then doth he propose
A stratagem, that makes the beldame start:
"A cruel man and impious thou art:
Sweet lady, let her pray, and sleep, and dream
Alone with her good angels, far apart
From wicked men like thee. Go, go [: by christ]!—I deem
Thou canst not surely be the same that thou didst seem."

STANZA 13: The stanza began differently: "He followed her
along a passage dark." Discuss the two versions of the opening line. Characterize the change in the last line, for example,
weak, strong expletive, and so forth. In line 5 we can see the
vision clarifying itself as Keats is describing not merely sce-
nery but a state of being as well.

STANZA 15: Madeline's situation is described more specifically in the final last line than earlier. Discuss this. Are there any changes of a similar nature in this stanza?

STANZA 16: The changes recorded here have to do with literary taste and decorum. The first change in line 2, however, may be of different substance. The first line earlier read: "Sudden a thought more rosy than the rose/Flush'd . . ." Discuss this change in emphasis.

1 7

"I will not harm her, by <u>all saints I swear</u>, [the great
    St. Paul;]"
Quoth Porphyro: "O may I ne'er find grace
When my weak voice shall <u>whisper its last prayer</u>, [unto
    heaven call]
If one of her soft ringlets I displace,
Or look with ruffian passion in her face:
Good Angela, <u>believe me by these tears</u>; [thou hearest
    how I swear]
Or I will, even in a moment's space,
   Awake, with horrid shout, my foemen's ears,
And beard them, though they be more fanged than wolves
    and bears."

1 8

"Ah! why <u>wilt thou</u> [will you] affright a feeble soul?
A poor, weak, palsy-stricken, churchyard thing,
Whose passing-bell may ere the <u>midnight</u> [morning] toll;
Whose prayers for thee, each morn and evening,
Were never missed."—Thus plaining, doth she bring
A gentler speech from burning Porphyro;
So <u>woeful</u> [gentle], and of such deep sorrowing,
That <u>Angela gives promise she will</u> [The old Beldam
    promises to] do
Whatever he shall wish, betide her weal or woe.

1 9

Which was, to <u>lead</u> [guide] him, in close secrecy,
Even to Madeline's chamber, and there hide
Him in a closet, <u>of such privacy</u> [if such one there be]
That he might see her beauty unespied,
And win perhaps that night a peerless bride,
While legioned faeries <u>paced the coverlet</u>, [round her
      pillow flew]
And pale enchantment held her sleepy-eyed.
<u>Never</u> [O when] on such a night have lovers met,
Since Merlin paid <u>his Demon</u> [the demons] all the monstrous
      debt.

2 0

"It shall be as thou wishest," said the Dame:
"All cates and dainties shall be storéd there
Quickly on this feast-night: by the tambour frame
Her own lute thou wilt see: no time to spare,
For I am slow and feeble, and scarce dare
On such a catering trust my dizzy head.
<u>Wait here, my child, with patience</u> [But wait an hour
      passing]; kneel in prayer
The while: Ah! thou must needs the lady wed,
Or may I never leave my grave among the dead."

STANZA 17: Note the care the poet takes with the question of swearing and by whom—one saint or many. What do such alterations suggest about the poet's conception of Porphyro and how does the developing action take shape from such considerations?

STANZA 19: The action of this stanza follows fast upon the one preceding. But an earlier development is revealed in the first attempt at an opening line: "Which was, as all who ever lov'd will guess." Comment on the two approaches to the action as it is eventually worked out. Do you recognize where certain changes have been made anticipating rhyming difficulties?

STANZA 20: This marks, in Professor Ridley's words, "almost
the last moment of easy composition in the poem . . ." He
continues: "But now, as the crisis of the action approaches,
the fever of composition increases, and one can study with
an excitement almost painful the workings of the creative
spirit in the throes of creation."

2 1

So saying, she hobbled off with busy fear.
The lover's endless minutes slowly passed;
The dame returned, and whispered in his ear
To follow her; with agéd eyes aghast
From fright of dim espial [any noise]. Safe at last,
Through many a dusky [lonely oaken] gallery, they gain
The maiden's chamber, silken, hushed, and chaste;
Where Porphyro took covert, pleased amain.
His poor guide hurried back with agues in her brain.

2 2

Her falt'ring [With fautling] hand upon the balustrade,
   [Ballustrad]
Old Angela was feeling for the stair, [Stair]
When Madeline, St. Agnes' charméd maid,
Rose, like a missioned spirit, [to her] unaware:
With silver [And with her] taper's light, and pious
   [gentle] care,
She turned, and down [led] the aged gossip led [down]
To a safe [the save] level matting. Now prepare,
Young Porphyro, for gazing [a-gazing] on that bed; [Bed]
She comes, she comes again, like ring-dove frayed and fled.

2 3

Out went the taper as she hurried [floated] in;
Its little smoke, in pallid moonshine, died;
She closed the door, she panted, all akin
To spirits of the air, and visions wide:
No uttered syllable, or, woe betide!

But to her heart, her heart was voluble,
Paining with eloquence her balmy side;
As though a tongueless nightingale should swell
Her throat in vain, and die, heart-stifled, in her dell.

2 4a

A Casement ach'd tripple archd and diamonded
With many coloured glass fronted the Moon
In midst <u>whereof</u> [of which] a shilded scutcheon shed
High <u>blushing</u> gules: upon she kneeled saintly down
And inly prayed for grace and heavenly boon
The blood red gules fell on her silver cross
And her white[st] hands devout

2 4

A casement high and triple-arched there was,
All <u>garlanded</u> [gardneded] with carven imag'ries
Of fruits, and flowers, and <u>bunches of knot-grass</u>, [sunny
    corn]
And diamonded with panes of quaint device,
Innumerable of stains and splendid <u>dyes</u>, [dies]
As are [is] the tiger-moth's <u>deep-damasked</u> [rich sunset]
    wings
And in the midst, 'mong <u>thousand</u> [man] heraldries,
And [dim] twilight saints, and <u>dim</u> emblazonings,
A shielded scutcheon blushed with <u>blood of queens and kings</u>.
    [Blood of Queens and Kings.]

STANZA 21: The earliest attempt at the first line reads like a
prose statement of what is to become poetry: "So saying she
hobbl'd out busily." And the simple but dramatic line 2 earlier
read: "And we will pass the Lover's endless hour;" What role
does poetic imagination play in the refining of this material?
Is the preferred version of line 5 much better than the original? If yes, why?

STANZA 22: This stanza was to continue Porphyro's story—
"There secreted,"—but the poet changed his mind and got
back to Angela. An early draft of the opening lines reads:

Scarce had old Angela the staircase found
Ere Madeline, like an affrightened Bird
Flew past her.

What problems can you discern here? Discuss the other revisions in this stanza.

STANZA 23: The last line, the Alexandrine, is a foot too long
in the first draft: "Her barren throat in vain and die heart
stifled in her dell." The "in vain" was first deleted, then
replaced for the final edition.

STANZA 24A: Discuss the fragment in light of the above.

STANZA 24: The stanza began "A Casement ach'd" and then
Keats made his image more elaborate, richer. Since the emotional stress is minimal and the action is at rest (for this and
the next stanza) the poet works with language as a painter
works with brush strokes. Though the narrative is in stasis
here, values take shape in these two stanzas. By noting the
revisions, demonstrate how those values evolve.

2 5

Full on this casement [Casement] shone the wintry moon,
And threw warm [red, rich] gules on Madeline's fair
        breast, [face]
As down she knelt [kneel'd] for heaven's grace and boon;
Rose-bloom fell on her [Tinging her pious] hands, to-
        gether prest,
And on her silver cross soft amethyst, [Amethyst]
And on her hair a glory, like a saint: [Saint's]
She seemed a splendid angel, newly drest, [like an im-
        mortal [silvery] angel drest,]
Save wings, for heaven:—Porphyro [Lionel] grew faint:
She knelt, so [too] pure a thing, so free from mortal taint.

26

Anon [But soon] his heart revives: her <u>vespers</u> [praying]
    <u>done</u>, [prayers said]
Of all its wreathed pearls her hair she <u>frees</u>; [strips]
Unclasps her <u>warmed</u> [bosom] jewels one by one;
Loosens her fragrant bodice; by degrees
Her <u>rich</u> [sweet] attire <u>creeps rustling</u> [falls light] to her
    knees:
Half-hidden, like a <u>mermaid in sea-weed</u>, [Syren of the
    Sea]
<u>Pensive awhile she dreams awake</u>, [She stands awhile in
    thought,] and sees
In fancy, fair St. Agnes in her bed,
But dares not look behind, or all the charm is <u>fled</u>. [dead]

27

Soon, trembling in her soft and chilly nest,
<u>In sort of wakeful swoon</u>, [She lay, in sort of wakeful
    swoon perplext] <u>perplexed she lay</u>,
Until the poppied warmth of sleep oppressed
Her soothéd <u>limbs</u>, [Limbs] and <u>soul</u> [Soul] fatigued
    away;
Flown, like a thought, until the morrow-day;
Blissfully haven'd both from joy and pain;
<u>Clasped</u> [Shut] like a missal where swart <u>Paynims</u> [pay-
    nims] pray;
<u>Blinded alike from</u> [Dead to] <u>sunshine</u> [Sunshine] and
    from rain,
As though a rose should <u>shut</u>, [close] and be a bud again.

28

Stol'n to this paradise, and so entranced,
Porphyro gazed upon her empty dress,
And <u>listened</u> [listen] to her breathing, if it chanced
To wake into slumberous tenderness;
Which when he heard, that minute did he bless,

And breathed himself: then from the closet crept,
Noiseless [Silent] as <u>fear</u> [Fear] in a <u>wide</u> [wild] wilder-
      ness,
And over the <u>hushed</u> [silent] carpet, <u>silent</u>, [hushing]
      stept,
And 'tween the <u>curtains</u> [Curtains] peeped, <u>where</u>, [and] lo!
      —how fast she slept.

STANZA 25: What in the fragment becomes extended in the
following stanza and to what effect? In other words, Keats,
by abandoning the moon imagery and the picture of Madeline
in stanza 24, allows himself working room in stanza 25.
Elaborate. The minor changes in line 7 create an interesting
effect. Discuss.

STANZA 26: Earlier Keats began this delicate and mildly erotic
passage with "she lays aside her veil," but we have nowhere
seen her veil and the poet is sure not to introduce extraneous
detail where none is needed. So the stanza proceeds with the
many starts and stops recorded above, indicating the complexity of the poetic process.
    Line 4 went through painful workings:

Loosens her bursting, her boddice from her
            her boddice lace string
            her boddice and her bosom bare
            her

The poet leaves off with an unfinished line. Later he writes:
"Loosens her fragrant bodice and doth bare/Her . . ." but gets
no further. He begins again moving toward the final vision:
"Loosens her fragrant boddice: and down slips/Her sweet
attire." For the further alteration of these lines view the
stanza. Can you account for these revisions?

STANZA 27: Earlier the stanza began: "The charm fled not—
she did not look behind;/Soon trembling . . . ." Why do you
think the poet deleted this opening in favor of the less transi-
tional line?

STANZA 28: Originally line 7 read: "Silent as Fear, and   ?
not with." Discuss the elaboration of this figure of
speech, the simile of fear. The question mark indicates Keats
at work.

29

Then [on] by the bed-side, where the faded moon [Moon]
Made a dim, silver [an illumed] twilight, soft he set
A table, and, half anguished, threw thereon [and with
    anguish spread theron]
A cloth [Cloth] of woven crimson, gold, and jet:—
O for some drowsy Morphean [morphean] amulet!
The boisterous, midnight, festive clarion, [of the Ball
    [feast]]
[Sounded though faint and far away]
The kettle-drum [And kettle-drums] and far-heard clari-
    net,
Affray his [Reach'd his scar'd] ears, though but in dying
    [with faintest] tone:—
The hall [Hall] door shuts again, and all the noise is [was]
    gone.

30

And [But] still she slept an azure-lidded sleep,
In blanchéd linen, smooth, and lavendered,
While he from forth the closet brought a heap
Of candied apple, quince, [fruits/sweets] and plum, and
    gourd;
With jellies soother than the creamy [dairy] curd,
And lucent syrups, tinct [smooth] with cinnamon;
[And sugar'd dates from that o'er Euphrates fard]
Manna and dates, in argosy [Brigantine] transferred
From Fez; and spicéd dainties, every one,
From silken [wealthy] [glutted] Samarcand to cedared Leb-
    anon. [lebanon]

3 1

These delicates he heaped with glowing hand
On golden dishes [salvers] and in baskets bright
Of wreathéd [twisted] silver: sumptuous they stand
In the retired quiet of the night,
Filling the chilly room with perfume light.—
"And now, my love [And now saith he], my seraph fair,
        awake!
Thou art my heaven, and I thine eremite:
Open thine eyes, for meek St. Agnes' sake,
Or I shall drowse beside thee, so my soul doth ache."

3 2

Thus whispering, his warm, unnervéd arm [s]
Sank in her pillow. Shaded was her dream [sleep]
        [dreams]
By the dusk curtains:—'twas a midnight charm [dream-
        less of alarms]
Impossible to melt as icéd stream:
The lustrous salvers in the moonlight gleam;
Broad golden fringe upon the carpet lies: [lies wealthy
        on the F]
It seemed he never, never could [can] redeem
From such a stedfast spell his lady's eyes;
So mused awhile, entoiled in wooféd phantasies.

STANZA 29: Line 3 originally read: "A table light, and stilly
threw theron." Discuss this line. Discuss Keats' handling of
tense in this stanza. What has the question of tense to do
with poetic values?

STANZA 30: Here we can observe the poet working with individual words to create the sensual effect of the feast. Discuss his choices.

STANZA 31: Line 4 earlier began: "Amid the quiet of St. Agnes' night,/And now saith he my seraph . . ." This would have begun the action of the stanza two lines earlier. What is the nature of the delay here? Is this a delay the structure of the stanza seems to determine? Discuss the deleted phrase in line 6.

STANZA 32: Discuss the shift in rhythm and tense in the stanza.

3 3

Awakening up, he took her hollow lute,—
Tumultuous,—and, in chords that tenderest be,
He played an ancient ditty, long since mute,
In Provence called, "La belle dame sans merci:"
Close to her ear touching [beheld] the melody;—
Wherewith disturbed, she utter'd a soft moan:
He ceased—she panted quick [her breathing ceas'd]—
    and suddenly
Her blue affrayéd [half-frayed] eyes wide open shone:
Upon his knees he sank, pale as smooth-sculptured stone.

3 4

Her eyes were open, but she still beheld,
Now wide awake, the vision of her sleep:
There was [some] a painful change, that nigh expelled
The blisses of her dream so pure and deep
At which fair Madeline began to weep,
And moan forth witless [little] words with many a sigh;
While still her gaze on Porphyro would keep;
Who knelt, with joinéd hands and piteous eye, [with an
    aching brow]
Fearing to move or speak, she looked so dreamingly.

3 5

"Ah, Porphyro!" said she, "but even now
Thy voice was at sweet tremble in [by] mine ear,

Made tuneable with every sweetest vow;
And <u>those sad</u> [thy kind] eyes were spiritual and clear:
How changed thou art! how pallid, chill, and drear!
Give me that voice again, my Porphyro,
Those looks immortal, those complainings dear!
Oh, leave me not in this eternal woe,
For if thou diest, my Love, I know not where to go."

3 6

Beyond a mortal man impassioned far
At these voluptuous <u>accents</u> [words], he arose,
Ethereal, flushed, and like a throbbing star
Seen mid the sapphire heaven's deep repose;
Into her dream he melted, as the rose
Blendeth <u>its odor</u> [her/its perfume] with the violet,—
Solution sweet: meantime the frost wind blows
Like Love's alarum pattering the sharp sleet
Against the <u>window panes</u> [casement gloom]; St. Agnes'
    moon hath set.

STANZA 33: Discuss the change in line 7.

STANZA 34: "Little" in line 6 may be more interesting than "witless." Discuss.

STANZA 36: The action of the poem is now mounting to its climax. The poet begins with a false start: "Impassion'd far beyond a mortal man." Line 5 was a struggle: "With her bright dream he . . ." and then: "In her bright dream he . . ." "Window dark" was an earlier possibility for the final line. Comment.

3 7

'Tis dark: <u>quick</u> [still] pattereth the flaw-blown sleet.
"This is no dream, my bride, my Madeline!"
'Tis dark: the iced gusts still rave and beat:
"No dream, alas! alas! and woe is mine!

Porphyro will leave me here to fade and pine.
[Ah] Cruel! what traitor could thee hither bring?
I curse not, for my heart is lost in thine,
Though thou forsakest a deceivéd thing;—
A dove forlorn and lost [A silent mateless dove] with sick
        unprunéd wing."

                            3 8

"My Madeline! sweet dreamer! lovely bride!
Say, may I be for aye thy vassal blest?
Thy beauty's shield, heart-shaped and vermeil-dyed?
Ah, silver shrine, here [by thee] will I take my rest
After so many hours of toil and quest,
A famished pilgrim,—saved by miracle.
Though I have found, I will not [cannot] rob thy nest,
Saving of thy sweet self; if thou think'st well
To trust, fair Madeline, to no rude infidel.

                            3 9

"Hark! 'tis an elfin-storm from faery land,
Of haggard seeming, but a boon indeed: [my love, to us]
Arise—arise [my love]! the morning is at hand;—
The bloated wassailers will never heed;—
Let us away, my love, with happy speed;
There are no ears to hear, or eyes to see,—
Drowned all in Rhenish and the sleepy [drench of] mead:
Awake! arise! my love, and fearless be,
For o'er the southern moors I have a home for thee."

                            4 0

She hurried at his words, beset with fears,
For there were sleeping dragons all around, [About]
At glaring watch, perhaps [Or perhaps at glaring . . .],
        with ready spears—
[well] Down the wide stairs a darkling way they found;
In all the house was heard no [not a] human sound.

A chain-drooped lamp was flickering <u>by each door</u>; [here
    and there]
The arras, <u>rich</u> [flutterd] with horseman, hawk, and
    hound,
Fluttered <u>in the besieging</u> [with cold] wind's uproar;
And the long carpets rose along the gusty floor.

STANZA 37: Line 8 was at one time conceived as line 9, the
longer Alexandrine: "Though thou should'st leave forsaken a
deceived thing." Ridley offers "wind" for "wing." What
special purpose does the longer line have in each stanza? Take
up the question of the Alexandrine in the context of this
stanza.

STANZA 38: This stanza was to open: "My Madeline! The
Dark is this wintry night." Rather, it begins with an impassioned apostrophe (address) to the heroine. Is there any need
for the natural description the deleted line begins to offer?

    Line 6 has a complicated evolution: "With tearful features
pale and mournful Pilgrim's weeds." This line is one foot too
long. Then it goes through: "Pale featured and in mournful
Pilgrims' weeds" to: "Pale featured and in weeds of Pil-
grimage."

STANZA 39: It is interesting that after line 5 Keats was about
to introduce a definite setting. He deleted "over the moors . . ."
What would this early introduction produce in the stanza?
The last two lines earlier read: "Put on warm clouthing sweet,
and fearless be/Over the bleak Dartmoor I have a home for
thee." There is a directness, a naturalness of diction to the
"put on warm clothing . . ." that is omitted in the final version. What different effects does such a change in language
produce? Is there an advantage to the less localized final
reading?

STANZA 40: Line 6 went through many attempts before the
final vision. The simple ideas fixed in this vision established
themselves:

The Lamps were flickering death shades on the walls
Without, the tempest kept a bellow roar
The Lamps were flickering
The Lamps were dying in
But here and there a Lamp was flickering out

41

They glide, like phantoms, into the wide hall;
Like phantoms, to the iron porch they glide,
Where lay [slept] the Porter, in uneasy sprawl,
With a huge [large] empty flagon [beaker] by his side:
The wakeful bloodhound rose, and shook his hide,
But his sagacious [unangered] eye an inmate owns:
By one, and one, the bolts full easy slide:—[easy bolts
        backslide]
The chains lie silent on the footworn stones; [Across the
        pavement lie the heavy chains]
The key turns, and the door upon its hinges groans.

42

And they are gone: aye, ages long ago
These lovers fled away into the storm. [into a night of
        storms]
That night the Baron dreamt of many a woe,
And all his warrior-guests with shade [shades] and
        form [forms]
Of witch, and demon, and large coffin-worm,
Were long be-nightmared. Angela the old
Died palsy-twitched, with meagre face deform;
The Beadsman, after thousand aves told,
For aye unsought-for slept among his ashes cold.

STANZA 41: The stanza began "Like Spirits into the wide-
paven hall/They glide, and to the iron porch in haste." In the
final version Keats has created a repetition of the central verb.
Beginning the stanza with this verb also heightens the movement of action.

Line 6 was originally: "And paced round Madeline all an-gerless." Discuss the evolution of this line and its changed effect.

STANZA 42: Discuss the difficulties with the word "night" in lines 2 and 3.

William Blake

1757—1827

Wᴵᴸᴸᴵᴬᴹ Bᴸᴬᴷᴱ, perhaps the first true Romantic poet, was largely neglected during his lifetime by both the public and critics, and it was not until forty years after his death that scholars began to take an interest in his life, his poetry, and his art. He epitomized what was later to become the Romantic ideal in his varied and individual genius. He was a lyric poet, as demonstrated by the *Songs of Innocence* and *Experience*; prophetic visionary, as exemplified by his mystical opus, "The Prophetic Books"; revolutionary, as expressed in *America, a Prophecy* and *The French Revolution;* and, in addition, artist and craftsman who illustrated and engraved the copper plates from which his poems were printed according to his own method of "illuminated printing."

Among those who did recognize his genius, the habitués of Joseph Johnson's bookshop, including the radical thinkers Thomas Paine, William Godwin, and Mary Wollstonecraft, there were few, if any, who could understand his ideas and the intense, abiding joy embedded in his mysticism. Blake's mysticism, influenced by the writings of Emmanuel Swedenborg, a religious mystic, teacher, scientist, and Neo-Platonist, eventually led him to repudiate doctrines of rationalism, systematic philosophy, and the orthodoxy of the Church. That is, he rejected all processes or methodologies that he felt interfered with man's direct apprehension of God and Truth. He was truly a free spirit, determined to liberate the body and soul:

Abstinence sows sand all over
The ruddy limbs & flaming hair,
But Desire Gratified
Plants fruits & beauty there.

Though Blake admired radical political and literary figures for their revolutionary temperament, libertarianism, and opposition to conformity, he believed their faith in rationalism and the benefits of science, law, analysis, and discipline separated them from the virtues of freedom. These virtues are symbolized by love, innocence, imaginativeness, and the primal unity with Spiritual Truth. In the childlike state of "unfallen mortality" these virtues are realized, but of course such an ideal state is impossible to maintain. The contrary state, the real as opposed to the ideal, is a part of life, and the light, laughter, and glee of the innocent state is tempered by the awareness of forthcoming experience, darkness, and evil. There are two sides to Blake's thought, and, indeed, for an understanding of his primary concern Dualism is necessary. His primary concern is with the finiteness of man compared to the whole universe and, ultimately, the correspondence of the material creation with man's spiritual insight to form a unity, or reality. The soul moves through a cycle of contrary states, good and evil. The Dualism though, even the darkness, arises from God, the Divine Reality. As Blake stated, "Without Contraries is no progression," and "To be in Error, and to be Cast out, is a part of God's design."

This chapter is made up of selections from the *Songs of Innocence* (1789), and the *Songs of Experience* (1794), poems that reflect the contraries of the human condition without presenting a systematic philosophy, but rather illustrating the ways in which the contrary states manifest themselves. Though it may not be apparent, if one considers these poems solely from the point of view of Blake's Dualistic ideas, these poems are masterpieces of simplicity and lyricism. Many of them have been put to music and have been sung. There is a certain tension in them, especially noticeable if one reads about the contrary states of a single subject, for example, God's creativity in "The Tyger" and "The Lamb." But this tension is the underlying human struggle for the recognition of ambiguities and, because of the very universality of this struggle, the poems, in expressing the tension, in no way lose their beauty, clarity, or simplicity.

In this chapter, each of the poems included from *Songs of Innocence* is presented along with a complement from *Songs of Experience*, with the exception of "London," which is from *Songs of Experience*. In a number of instances, there are first drafts or first versions as well. This is in exception to the general format of the book, which concentrates on different versions alone. Here the reason for giving two different poems instead of only versions of a single poem is to emphasize that there may be multiple approaches to a particular conception, idea, or experience and again, to permit the reader to accept this idea even when confronted with B and C versions of a single poem. This is an attempt to blur the concept of versions of poems with that of separate poems, for each different creation, even variants, requires separate attention.

The text used, along with *Songs of Innocence* and *Songs of Experience*, is Sir Geoffrey Keynes's *Complete Writings of William Blake* (1957), which contains all the variant readings. Two more recent studies of Blake's *Songs* are D. G. Gellhorn's *Blake's Contrary States* (1966) and E. D. Hirsch's *Innocence and Experience: An Introduction to Blake* (1964).

A

Introduction

Piping down the valleys wild,
Piping song of pleasant glee,
On a cloud I saw a child,
And he laughing said to me:

"Pipe a song about a Lamb!"   5
So I piped with merry cheer.
"Piper, pipe that song again;"
So I piped: he wept to hear.

"Drop thy pipe, thy happy pipe;
Sing thy songs of happy cheer:"   10

So I sung the same again,
While he wept with joy to hear.

"Piper, sit thee down and write
In a book, that all may read."
So he vanish'd from my sight,   15
And I pluck'd a hollow reed,

And I made a rural pen,
And I stain'd the water clear,
And I wrote my happy songs
Every child may joy to hear.   20

             Songs of Innocence

A

Introduction

Hear the voice of the Bard!
Who Present, Past, & Future, sees;
Whose ears have heard
The Holy Word
That walk'd among the ancient trees,   5

Calling the lapsed Soul,
And weeping in the evening dew;
That mighty controll
The starry pole,
And fallen, fallen light renew!   10

"O Earth, O Earth, return!
Arise from out the dewy grass;
Night is worn,
And the morn
Rises from the slumberous mass.   15

"Turn away no more;
Why wilt thou turn away?
The starry floor,
The wat'ry shore,
Is giv'n thee till the break of day."   20

   Songs of Experience

   1. Both poems contain a note of optimism. How is this attitude directed in each instance?

   2. The poet acts as hero or main figure in both poems. Yet clearly his poetic function is different in the two contexts. In the *Songs of Experience* Introduction the context is a religious one with the bard as a God-inspired man and the voice of prophecy. He is calling to Adam, if we follow that symbolic association, as he is affirming the cyclical order in the natural world. Discuss the poet's role in the *Songs of Innocence* Introduction.

   3. In the earlier poem the language is direct, almost childlike. The repetition and simplicity of design suggest the innocence of childhood. The control evident in the poem, however, is not youthful and should indicate the association of the piper with the wise and watchful innocence of Christ. The figure of Christ dominates the *Songs of Innocence* and acts as a bridge or unifier between the helpless child and the wise poet-adult.

   4. A dramatic form is used in both of these songs. The drama is more clearly felt between the child and the piper, however, than in the song of experience. Discuss dialogue and dramatic expectancy in both poems.

A

The Lamb

Little Lamb, who made thee?
Dost thou know who made thee?
Gave thee life, & bid thee feed
By the stream & o'er the mead;
Gave thee clothing of delight,   5
Softest clothing, wooly, bright;
Gave thee such a tender voice,
Making all the vales rejoice?
Little Lamb, who made thee?
Dost thou know who made thee?   10

Little Lamb, I'll tell thee,
Little Lamb, I'll tell thee:
He is called by thy name,
For he calls himself a Lamb.
He is meek, & he is mild;   15
He became a little child.
I a child, & thou a lamb,
We are called by his name.
Little Lamb, God bless thee!
Little Lamb, God bless thee!   20

Songs of Innocence

B

The Tyger

Tyger, Tyger, burning bright
In the forests of the night,
What immortal hand or eye
[Could] [Dare] frame thy fearful symmetry?

Dare, then, was a primary intention held off till the end only to increase the effect

[In what] [Burnt in] distant deeps or skies   5
[Burnt the] [The cruel] fire of thine eyes?   *too sing-songish*
On what wings dare he aspire?
What the hand dare seize the fire?

And what shoulder & what art
Could twist the sinews of thy heart?   10
And when thy heart began to beat
What dread hand & what dread feet

[Could fetch it from the furnace deep ⟍   *elimination of*
And in thy horrid ribs dare steep   ⎫   *syntactical sensepatern*
∞ —In the well of sanguine woe?   ⎬   15
In what clay & in what mould   ⎭
Were thy eyes of fury roll'd?] ⟋

[What] Where the hammer? [What] Where the chain?
In what furnace was thy brain?
What the anvil? What [the arm] [arm] [grasp] [clasp]
fuller _dread_ grasp?   *stronger* 20
[Could] Dare its deadly terrors [grasp] clasp?

Tyger, Tyger, burning bright
In the forests of the night,   *finally, more input*
What immortal hand & eye
Dare [form] frame thy fearful symmetry? — *finally)*   25

(3) And [did he laugh] dare he [smile] [laugh] his work
        to see?   *less child-like*
    [What the (shoulder) ankle? What the knee?] ————— /
(4) [Did] Dare he who made the lamb make thee?   '
(1) When the stars threw down their spears
(2) And water'd heaven with their tears *romantical last line*

    Note-book, 1793

A

The Tyger

Tyger! Tyger! burning bright
In the forests of the night,
What immortal hand or eye
Could frame thy fearful symmetry?

In what distant deeps or skies   5
Burnt the fire of thine eyes?
On what wings dare he aspire?
What the hand dare seize the fire?

And what shoulder, & what art.
Could twist the sinews of thy heart?   10
And when thy heart began to beat,
What dread hand? & what dread feet?

What the hammer? what the chain?
In what furnace was thy brain?
What the anvil? what dread grasp   15
Dare its deadly terrors clasp?

When the stars threw down their spears,
And water'd heaven with their tears,
Did he smile his work to see?
Did he who made the Lamb make thee?   20

Tyger! Tyger! burning bright
In the forests of the night,
What immortal hand or eye,
Dare frame thy fearful symmetry?

Songs of Experience

1. "The Lamb" is one of a number of songs that incor-
porate a question-answer method. Here the questioner and

the one questioned are identical. How is this identity made manifest?

2. Note that couplets open and close each stanza. They contain three stresses (the emphasis given to a syllable or word in rhythmic writing) each. Can you detect the difference in rhythm in the central couplets? The contrast in rhythm parallels other contrasting elements in the poem. Comment.

3. "The Tyger" demonstrates Blake's great art of the lyric. The language is lively and simple yet there is immense complexity and ambiguity of meaning. Compare "forests of the night" with "clothing of delight." Both are highly suggestive; they are not different kinds of phrases, yet one is more complex in thought and tone.

4. Unlike "The Lamb" in the *Songs of Innocence*, "The Tyger" answers none of its own questions. Here the questions are rhetorical, that is, the grand and ultimate answers are implicit in the questions themselves. Demonstrate and discuss.

5. "The Tyger," in its acceptance of the terror of life is, in part, a satire of "The Lamb," which excludes what is fearful from our experience. In the song of experience terror may be positive. The illusion that the poem satirizes is that in a state of innocence fear and terror are emotions that can and should be transcended. The Tyger is as natural, as fundamental as the Lamb. The satire is not the biting kind, for Blake wants not to mock the Lamb but to combine the positive forces of experience with it.

6. Note in the B version of "The Tyger" such canceled phrases as "cruel fire," "horrid ribs," and "sanguine woe." How do such phrases interfere with the powerful affirmative motif in the poem?

7. The notebook version demonstrates a shifting around of stanzas and lines within the stanzas as well. It is most interesting to perceive Blake's hesitancy with individual key words. In the draft he occasionally preferred words that were later changed back to the original version, namely, lines 18, 21 and 28.

A

The Chimney Sweeper

When my mother died I was very young,
And my father sold me while yet my tongue
Could scarcely cry " 'weep! 'weep! 'weep! 'weep!"
So your chimneys I sweep, & in soot I sleep.

There's little Tom Dacre, who cried when his head   5
That curl'd like a lamb's back, was shav'd: so I said
"Hush, Tom! never mind it, for when your head's bare
You know that the soot cannot spoil your white hair."

And so he was quiet, & that very night,
As Tom was a-sleeping, he had such a sight!   10
That thousands of sweepers, Dick, Joe, Ned, & Jack,
Were all of them lock'd up in coffins of black.

And by came an Angel who had a bright key,
And he open's the coffins & set them all free;
Then down a green plain leaping, laughing, they run   15
And wash in a river, and shine in the Sun.

Then naked & white, all their bags left behind,
They rise upon clouds and sport in the wind;
And the Angel told Tom, if he'd be a good boy,
He'd have God for his father, & never want joy.   20

And so Tom awoke; and we rose in the dark,
And got with our bags & our brushes to work.
Tho' the morning was cold, Tom was happy & warm;
So if they all do their duty they need not fear harm.

Songs of Innocence

$\mathcal{A}$

The Chimney Sweeper

A little black thing among the snow,
Crying " 'weep! 'weep!" in notes of woe!
"Where are thy father & mother? say?"
"They are both gone up to the church to pray.

"Because I was happy upon the heath,   5
And smil'd among the winter's snow,
They clothed me in the clothes of death,
And taught me to sing the notes of woe.

"And because I am happy & dance & sing
They think they have done me no injury,   10
And are gone to praise God & his Priest & King,
Who make up a heaven of our misery."

Songs of Experience

1. In the song of innocence the sweep is an orphan. In the later poem no such detail is given. There Blake presents his victim of social injustice exclusively as an object of exploitation. Discuss the poet's role as reformer in the one poem and his avoidance of such questions in the other. In his role as reformer how does he employ satire to attack the complacency of the first poem?

2. Discuss Tom Dacre's function in the first song and his absence in the second.

3. Despite his woe, Tom Dacre is made happy as a vision descends upon him. The sweep in the shorter poem is happy too, for he recognizes (maybe not consciously) the strength of life and the union with nature (lines 5 and 6) that lies within him. Despite the song of experience's satire, how is Tom's vision affirmed in both poems?

4. Taking a clue from the word "thing" in line 1 of the song of experience, discuss the different approaches to life's misery and sorrow in the two poems.

5. In the first draft version of this song of experience from
the 1793 Note-book there is an interesting variant for the last
line: "Who wrap themselves up in our misery." Comment on
this and the revised line 12.

A

The Little Boy Lost

"Father! father! where are you going?
O do not walk so fast.
Speak, father, speak to your little boy,
Or else I shall be lost."

The night was dark, no father was there;   5
The child was wet with dew;
The mire was deep, & the child did weep,
And away the vapour flew.

> *Songs of Innocence*

B

· · ·

["Then] And father [I cannot] how can I love you   5
[Nor] Or any of my brothers more?
I love [myself, so does the bird]
    you like the little bird
That picks up crumbs around the door."

The Priest sat by and heard the child.
In trembling zeal he siez'd his hair: 10
[The mother follow'd, weeping aloud:
"O, that I such a fiend should bear."]
[Then] He led him by his little coat

[To show his zealous, priestly care.]
And all admir'd his priestly care.   15

.   .   .

The weeping child could not be heard;   20
The weeping parents wept in vain.
[They bound his little ivory limbs
In a cruel Iron chain.]
[And] They strip'd him to his little shirt
& bound him in an iron chain.   25

[They] And burn'd him in a holy [fire] place,

> Stanzas selected from first draft of "A Little Boy Lost,"
> in *Songs of Experience*, Note-book (1793).

A

A Little Boy Lost

"Nought loves another as itself,
Nor venerates another so,
Nor is it possible to Thought
A greater than itself to know:

"And Father, how can I love you   5
Or any of my brothers more?
I love you like the little bird
That picks up crumbs around the door."

The Priest sat by and heard the child,
In trembling zeal he siez'd his hair: 10
He led him by his little coat,
And all admir'd the Priestly care.

And standing on the altar high,
"Lo! what a fiend is here!" said he,
"One who sets reason up for judge   15
Of our most holy Mystery."

The weeping child could not be heard,
The weeping parents wept in vain;
They strip'd him to his little shirt,
And bound him in an iron chain;   20

And burn'd him in a holy place,
Where many had been burn'd before:
The weeping parents wept in vain.
Are such things done on Albion's shore?

> *Songs of Experience*

1. Is Blake implying, in the last words of the song of innocence, that a child's weeping is magical and affirmative?
"Vapour" could be construed as mere nothingness, illusion.
How would this understanding of the word illuminate the
poem's ambiguous close?

2. Line 5 of the song of innocence suggests the orphan
motif we have already seen in "The Chimney Sweeper." With
no father the little boy adopts God the Father as his own in a
very human sense. Note how this developing idea prepares
us for the experience poem.

3. In the song of experience the little boy is not lost in the
dark, but is lost to the world after the sacrificial fire. Here,
unlike most of the contrary poems, there is no satire or parody
offered to the song of innocence. This poem may not have
been originally intended for *Songs of Experience*. The title
came last and it was not etched for the original issue of the
Songs of Experience.

4. The ironic spirit of experience (namely, line 12) is opposed to innocence. Discuss.

5. The little boy in both poems is innocent and, therefore,
must speak the truth. What kind of truth is spoken in the
song of experience and how does such truth infuriate the
Priest? The child is clearly a religious martyr. In what way is
his religion subversive?

6. Note how in the early draft the developing idea of self-
love was carried into line 7. Is the idea clearer and more
emphatic in the earlier draft?

7. Note the interesting change in line 11. Discuss.

8. There is a loss in graphic detail by the deletion of line 22. Does this change, in any way, improve the poem? How does it alter our vision of the particular experience in this stanza?

A

Holy Thursday

'Twas on a Holy Thursday, their innocent faces clean,
The children walking two & two, in red & blue & green,
Grey-headed beadles walk'd before, with wands as white
      as snow,
Till into the high dome of Paul's they like Thames' waters
    flow.

O what a multitude they seem'd, these flowers of London
      town!   5
Seated in companies they sit with radiance all their own.
The hum of multitudes was there, but multitudes of lambs,
Thousands of little boys & girls raising their innocent hands.

Now like a mighty wind they raise to heaven the voice
      of song,
Or like harmonious thunderings the seats of Heaven
      among.   10
Beneath them sit the aged men, wise guardians of the poor;
Then cherish pity, lest you drive an angel from your door.

    Songs of Innocence

A

Holy Thursday

Is this a holy thing to see
In a rich and fruitful land,
Babes reduc'd to misery,
Fed with cold and usurous hand?

Is that trembling cry a song?   5
Can it be a song of joy?
And so many children poor?
It is a land of poverty!

And their sun does never shine,
And their fields are bleak & bare,   10
And their ways are fill'd with thorns:
It is eternal winter there.

For where-e'er the sun does shine,
And where-e'er the rain does fall,
Babe can never hunger there,   15
Nor poverty the mind appall.

Songs of Experience

1. The song of innocence is set in London, as was "The Chimney Sweeper." Authenticity is sought after through the inclusion of various physical details. Discuss setting and naturalistic detail in both the song of innocence and the song of experience.

2. By placing the "aged men" (usually guardians-shepherds) "beneath" the children (lambs—to be guarded) Blake has turned the religious order upside down. Such a perversion of natural order is prepared for throughout the poem. Discuss.

3. The experience poem is clearly a parody or satire of the earlier poem. Discuss the development of images in both songs. Has the imagined perception of the experience poem

suffered from the social indignation or partisanship of its
attack? Where are the sympathies concrete; where are they
abstract?

4. Discuss complexity and simplicity in both of the songs.

5. Line 7 of the 1793 draft of the song of experience read
"And so great a number poor?" Discuss this deletion.

A

Infant Joy

"I have no name:
I am but two days old."
What shall I call thee?
"I happy am,
Joy is my name."   5
Sweet joy befall thee!

Pretty joy!
Sweet joy but two days old,
Sweet joy I call thee:
Thou dost smile,   10
I sing the while,
Sweet joy befall thee!

Songs of Innocence

B

· · ·

When I saw that rage was vain,
And to sulk would nothing gain,   10
[I began to so] [Seeking many an artful wile]
Turning many a trick & wile,
I began to soothe & smile.

And I [grew] [smil'd] sooth'd day after day
Till upon the ground I stray: 15
And I [grew] smil'd night after night,
Seeking only for delight.

[But upon the nettly ground
No delight was to be found]
And I saw before me shine   20
Clusters of the wand'ring vine
[And beyond a mirtle tree]
And many a lovely flower & tree
Stretch'd [its] their blossoms out to me.

[But a] [But many a Priest]   25
My father then with holy look,
In [their] his hands a holy book,
Pronounc'd curses on [his] my head
[Who the fruit or blossoms shed]
And bound me in a mirtle shade.   30

[I beheld the Priests by night;
They embrac'd [my mirtle] the blossoms bright:
I beheld the Priests by day;
[Where beneath my]
Underneath the vines [he] they lay]   35

[(3) Like [a] to serpents in the night,
  (4) They [*altered to* He] embrac'd my [mirtle] blossoms
            bright]
  (1) Like [a] to [serpents in the] holy men by day,
  (2) Underneath [my] the vines [he] they lay.

So I smote them & [his] their gore   40
Stain'd the roots my mirtle bore;
But the time of youth is fled,
And grey hairs are on my head.

From the first draft of "Infant Sorrow," Note-book (1793)

A

Infant Sorrow

My mother groaned, my father wept;
Into the dangerous world I leapt,
Helpless, naked, piping loud,
Like a fiend hid in a cloud.

Struggling in my father's hands   5
Striving against my swaddling bands,
Bound & weary, I thought best
To sulk upon my mother's breast.

    Songs of Experience

1. Stanza 1 of "Infant Joy" is a dialogue and the second,
a song sung by the adult. How are these different forms inte-
grated? Note how the parts of the dialogue are not separated
by "she said" or "the child replied." How are empathy and
parental (maternal) love expressed through the combined
form?

2. Is there an acknowledgment of sorrow or fearfulness in
the word "befall"? Explain.

3. Originally "Infant Sorrow" was a much longer poem. It
is printed here as B without the first two stanzas which later
became the song of experience. The shortened version is more
clearly polemical or contrary to the song of innocence. Regarding B, show how the first two stanzas act as an introduction to a history of the speaker from birth to old age.

4. These two short songs belong together as do "The Lamb"
and "The Tyger." While the song of experience does offer
ironic or satiric commentary to the earlier song it also comple-
ments it by demonstrating the human need for a balanced
view. The willfulness, vigor, and sorrow of the song of experience is as much a part of Blake's world view as the passive
loveliness of "Infant Joy." What the song of experience does

satirize is a one-sided view of man and the human condition.
Illustrate.

5. In view of "The Tyger," how is "dangerous" (line 2 of
"Infant Sorrow") a positive word? Discuss the affirmative
nature of the full version of "Infant Sorrow."

B

London

I wander thro' each dirty street,
Near where the dirty Thames does flow,
And [see] mark in every face I meet
Marks of weakness, marks of woe.

In every cry of every man   5
In [every voice of every child]
      every infant's cry of fear
In every voice, in every ban
The [german] mind forg'd [links I hear] manacles I hear.

[But most] How the chimney sweeper's cry
[Blackens o'er the churches' walls]   10
Every black'ning church appalls,
And the hapless soldier's sigh
Runs in blood down palace walls.

[But most the midnight harlot's curse
From every dismal street I hear,   15
Weaves around the marriage hearse
And blasts the new born infant's tear.]

But most [from every] thro' wintry streets I hear
How the midnight harlot's curse
Blasts the new born infant's tear,   20
And [hangs] smites with plagues the marriage hearse.

But most the shrieks of youth I hear
But most thro' midnight & . . . .
How the youthful . . .

Note-book (1793)

A

London

I wander thro' each charter'd street,
Near where the charter'd Thames does flow,
And mark in every face I meet
Marks of weakness, marks of woe.

In every cry of every Man,   5
In every Infant's cry of fear,
In every voice, in every ban,
The mind-forg'd manacles I hear.

How the Chimney-sweeper's cry
Every black'ning Church appalls;   10
And the hapless Soldier's sigh
Runs in blood down Palace walls.

But most thro' midnight streets I hear
How the youthful Harlot's curse
Blasts the new born Infant's tear,   15
And blights with plagues the Marriage hearse.

1. This great poem is about human squalor and misery
peculiar to large cities, yet it is not indicting London itself.
Blake's scathing ironies are reserved for man in a graceless
state. He is against the chartering of human lives, which is to
say, he is against slavery and tyranny in all their institutional
manifestations. To charter is to "hire out." How is this a more
appropriate word than the earlier "dirty"? How can the
Thames, a free-flowing river, be "chartered"?

2. Discuss verbal daring generally in this poem. Use the B version to illuminate Blake's care with phrasing and individual words.

3. The poem offers revolutionary faith that the human spirit may be transformed. What is needed is the removal of institutional tyrannies. As if these institutions are not explicit enough in this poem, Blake offers a fragment from the Rossetti Manuscript, no. 33:

Remove away that black'ning church:
Remove away that marriage hearse:
Remove away that man of blood
You'll quite remove the ancient curse.

A Miscellany
of Poets

THIS last chapter differs from the preceding ones in two ways. Rather than containing the poetry of one major poet, it presents a variety of poets with a few examples of each of their work. The second departure is that, with a few exceptions, I have left off commenting on the variant readings of the poems. The reader will find here two or more versions of a poem and will proceed with his own comparative analysis. At this point, the questioning method should be part of the reader's natural approach to poetry. Asking specific questions about specific changes is a good first step into larger questions and perceptions about poetry in general.

In the case of the single poem by Marianne Moore, the two versions are so interestingly different that I felt a need to say a few words. I am sure the reader will want to go further.

In no case here do the poems offered for attention represent what could be called the center or full achievement of that poet's work. These selections were not meant to be representative, but rather they were chosen for their utility in studying poetic revision.

WILLIAM SHAKESPEARE

1564–1616

The *Sonnets* of William Shakespeare were published in 1609. The B version presented here is from that publication and the one most likely taken from Shakespeare's own manuscript. The alterations in punctuation and spelling came in a later edition. This "corrected" version, the A version here, is the one most readers have read and taken as the final form. Ulti-

mately, the reader should not be overly concerned with which
version comes closest to Shakespeare's original (after all, the
1609 edition may have contained errors, as Shakespeare was
not likely to have seen the proofs); rather, the reader should
find it interesting to study punctuation and spelling as it affects the total effect of the poem.

B

Th' expence of Spirit in a waste of shame
Is lust in action, and till action, lust
Is perjurd, murdrous, blouddy full of blame,
Sauage, extreame, rude, cruell, not to trust,
Inioyd no sooner but dispised straight,　　　　　　　　　5
Past reason hunted, and sooner had
Past reason hated as a swollowed bayt,
On purpose layd to make the taker mad.
Made In pursut and in possession so,
Had, hauing, and in quest, to haue extreame,　　　　　10
A blisses in proofe and proud and very wo,
Before a ioy proposed behind a dreame,
　　　All this the world well knowes yet none knowes well,
　　　To shun the heauen that leads men to this hell.

A

Sonnet 129

Th' expense of Spirit in a waste of shame
Is lust in action; and till action, lust
Is perjured, murderous, bloody, full of blame,
Savage, extreme, rude, cruel, not to trust;
Enjoy'd no sooner but despised straight;　　　　　　5
Past reason hunted; and, no sooner had,
Past reason hated, as a swallow'd bait
On purpose laid to make the taker mad:
Mad in pursuit, and in possession so;

Had, having, and in quest to have, extreme;   10
A bliss in proof, and proved, a very woe;
Before, a joy proposed; behind, a dream.
    All this the world well knows; yet none knows well
    To shun the heaven that leads men to this hell.

MATTHEW ARNOLD

1822–1888

Matthew Arnold is mainly considered the outstanding literary
and social critic of the Victorian period in England. While his
name must rank behind the two major Victorian poets, Browning and Tennyson, his achievement as a poet is certainly con-
siderable. "Philomela" and "Dover Beach" number among the
most anthologized of English poems. "Quiet Work" is an
example of Arnold's earlier poetry.

Arnold published his first book of poems at the age of 26
and by the time he was 32, three volumes later, he was mostly
finished writing poetry and was turning to prose criticism.
Through his criticism he was to achieve the status of guide to
his age. This quality of guide or sage is also present in the
poetry.

B

Quiet Work

Two lessons, Nature, let me learn of thee,
Two lessons that in every wind are blown;
Two blending duties, harmonis'd in one,
Though the loud world proclaim their enmity—

Of toil unsever'd from tranquility!   5
Of labour, that in one short hour outgrows
Man's noisy schemes, accomplish'd in repose,
Too great for haste, too high for rivalry!

Yes, while on earth a thousand discords ring,
Man's weak complainings mingling with his toil,   10
Still do thy sleepless ministers move on,
Their glorious course in silence perfecting;
Still working, chiding still our vain turmoil,
Labourers that shall not fail, when man is gone.

Additional alternatives:

l.3: two duties serv'd in one/kept in one [at one]
l.6: that in still advance outgrows/that in fruit by far out-
     goes [by far outgrows] [in lasting fruit outgrows]
l.7: Man's noisy feats [work]
l.10: Man's senseless uproar/Our senseless uproar mingling
      with our toil,/Man's senseless uproar mingling with
      his toil,
l.11: quiet ministers

A

Quiet Work

One lesson, Nature, let me learn of thee,
One lesson which in every wind is blown,
One lesson of two duties kept at one
Though the loud world proclaim their enmity—

Of toil unsever'd from tranquility!   5
Of labour, that in lasting fruit outgrows
Far noisier schemes, accomplish'd in repose,
Too great for haste, too high for rivalry!

Yes, while on earth a thousand discords ring,
Man's fitful uproar mingling with his toil,   10
Still do thy sleepless ministers move on,
Their glorious tasks in silence perfecting;
Still working, blaming still our vain turmoil,
Labourers that shall not fail, when man is gone.

B

Philomela

Hark! ah, the nightingale—
The inken throated!
Hast thou not yet, poor bird
Been help'd by slipping years
At least to half forgetfulness   5
Of that old pain.
Can change of scene, and night,
And moonlight, & the dew,
And these frail acacia [blanch'd song-stirr'd] boughs
Thro whose frail [light] leaves, & showers   10
Of blossom'd clusters pale,
Thy voice in [by] gushes comes,
To thy torn heart and brain
Afford no balm?
Dost thou still behold   15
Here, through the moonlight on this English grass,
The unfriendly palace in the Thracian wild?
Dost thou still peruse
In the white acacia flowers
With hot cheeks and sear'd eyes   20
The too clear web, and thy dumb sister's shame?
Dost thou still reach
Thy husband, weak avenger, thro thyself?
Dost thou once more assay
Thy flight, and feel come over thee,   25
Poor fugitive, the feathery change
Once more, and once more seem to make resound
With love and hate, triumph and agony,
Lone Daulis, and the high Cephissian vale?
Hark, hark, Eugenia!   30
How thick the bursts come crowding through the leaves!
Once more—thou hearest?
Eternal passion!
Eternal pain!

A

Philomela

Hark, ah, the nightingale—
The tawny-throated!
Hark, from that moonlit cedar what a burst!
What triumph! hark!—what pain!

O wanderer from a Grecian shore,   5
Still, after many years, in distant lands,
Still nourishing in thy bewilder'd brain
That wild, unquench'd, deep-sunken, old-world pain—
Say, will it never heal?
And can this fragrant lawn   10
With its cool trees, and night,
And the sweet, tranquil Thames,
And moonshine, and the dew,
To thy rack'd heart and brain
Afford no balm?   15
Dost thou to-night behold,
Here, through the moonlight on this English grass,
The unfriendly palace in the Thracian wild?
Dost thou again peruse
With hot cheeks and sear'd eyes   20
The too clear web, and thy dumb sister's shame?
Dost thou once more assay
Thy flight, and feel come over thee,
Poor fugitive, the feathery change
Once more, and once more seem to make resound   25
With love and hate, triumph and agony,
Lone Daulis, and the high Cephissian vale?
Listen, Eugenia—
How thick the bursts come crowding through the leaves!
Again—thou hearest?   30
Eternal passion!
Eternal pain!

A

Dover Beach

The sea is calm to-night.
The tide is full, the moon lies fair
Upon the straits;—on the French coast the light
Gleams [Shines] and is gone; the cliffs of England stand,
Glimmering and vast, out in the tranquil bay.   5
Come to the window, sweet [hush'd] is the night-air!
Only, from the long line of spray
Where the sea [ebb] meets the moon-blanch'd land,
Listen! you hear the grating roar
Of pebbles which the waves draw [suck] back, and fling,   10
At their return, up the high [steep/barr'd] strand,
Begin, and cease, [Cease and begin] and then again begin,
With tremulous [regular/mournful] cadence slow, and bring
The eternal note of sadness in.

Sophocles long ago   15
Heard it on the Aegean, and it brought
Into his mind the turbid [troubled] ebb and flow
Of human misery; we
Find also in the sound a thought,
Hearing it by this distant northern sea.   20

The Sea of Faith
Was once, too, at the full, and round earth's shore
Lay like the folds of a bright girdle [garment] furl'd.
But now I [we] only hear
Its melancholy, long, withdrawing roar,   25
Retreating, to the breath
Of the night-wind, down the vast edges drear
And naked shingles of the world.

Ah, love, let us be true
To one another! for the world, which seems   30
To lie before us like a land of dreams,
So various, so beautiful, so new,

Hath really neither joy, nor love, nor light,
Nor certitude, nor peace, nor help for pain;
And we are here as on a darkling plain   35
Swept with confused alarms of struggle and flight, [fight]
Where ignorant armies clash by night.

GERARD MANLEY HOPKINS

1844–1889

Gerald Manley Hopkins was a poet and Jesuit priest. His poetry is charged with a religious, indeed, a mystical fervor. His
ideas and feelings about the new kind of poetry he was writing in the 1870's and 1880's are recorded in his correspondence
with his friend and later his literary editor Robert Bridges.

C

The Windhover*

I caught this morning morning's minion, king
    Of daylight's dauphin, dapple-dawn-drawn Fal-
        con—he was riding
        [con, riding]
        [Rolling]
        Rolling level underneath him steady air, and striding
        Hung
        [:Hung]
[He hung] so and rung the rein of a wimpled wing
In an ecstacy; then off, : forth on swing,
    As a skate's heel sweeps smooth on a bow-
        -bend: the hurl and gliding
[Rebuffed the big : wind. My heart]
        in

---

* A prose note by Hopkins read, "Sprung [Falling] paeonic rhythm,
sprung and outriding."

Rebuffed the big : wind. My heart in hiding
: Stirred for a bird—for the master of the thing!

Brute beauty and valour and act, O air, pride, plume,
       here
       Buckle! And the fire that breaks from thee then, a billion
[Times to]
: Times told lovelier, more dangerous, O my chevalier!

No wonder of it : sheer : plod makes plough down sillion
       : Shine, and blue-bleak embers, ah, my dear,
Fall, gall themselves, and gash : gold-vermilion.

B

I caught this morning morning's minion, king
       Of daylight's dauphin, dapple-dawn-drawn Falcon,
          in his riding
       Of the rolling level underneath him steady air, and
          striding
: O how he rung upon the rein of a wimpling wing
In his ecstacy! then off, : forth on swing,
       As a skate's heel sweeps smooth on a bow-bend:
          the hurl and gliding
       Rebuffed the big : wind. My heart in hiding
: Stirred for a bird—for the mastery of the thing!

A

The Windhover:

TO CHRIST OUR LORD

I caught this morning morning's minion, king-
       dom of daylight's dauphin, dapple-dawn-drawn Falcon, in
             his riding
       Of the rolling level underneath him steady air, and striding
High there, how he rung upon the rein of a wimpling wing

In his ecstacy! then off, off forth on swing,   5
  As a skate's heel sweeps smooth on a bow-bend: the hurl
     and gliding
  Rebuffed the big wind. My heart in hiding
Stirred for a bird,—the achieve of, the mastery of the thing!

Brute beauty and valour and act, oh, air, pride, plume here
  Buckle! AND the fire that breaks from thee then, a billion 10
Times told lovelier, more dangerous, O my chevalier!

  No wonder of it: shéer plód makes plough down sillion
Shine, and blue-bleak embers, ah my dear,
  Fall, gall themselves, and gash gold-vermilion.

D. H. LAWRENCE

1885–1930

Although D. H. Lawrence's reputation rests on his fiction
more than on his poetry, the two are essentially related. He
was a revolutionary artist and a moralist, who applied the
teachings of Freud, among other influences, to literary works
of art. In both his fiction and his poetry, Lawrence was
championing a moral program which would, if put into action, cure an age of diseases almost too terrible to define.

The poem "Man's Image" is a good example of how
Lawrence often uses poetry to develop a doctrine. "Bavarian
Gentians," a truly fine poem, not marred by Lawrence's urge
to convert his readers to his own moral system—as are many
of his poems—contains much of the best he was able to
achieve. Here the flowers are clearly symbolic and the speaker
in the poem can easily be seen as a hero who is able to
transcend the world of petty and corrupt values and merge
with natural forces.

B

Renaissance

We have bit no forbidden apple—
Eve and me—
Yet the splashes of day and night
Falling round us no longer dapple
The same Eden with purple and white.   5

This our own still valley
My Eden, my home
But the day shows it vivid with feeling
And the pallor of night does not tally
With the dark sleep that once covered the ceiling.   10

My little red heifer—go and look at her eyes—
She will calve tomorrow—
Take the lantern, and watch the Sow, for fear she grab her
        new litter
With red snarling jaws; let yourself listen to the cries
Of the new-born, and the unborn; and the old owl and the
        bats as they flitter   15
And wake to the sound of the woodpigeons, and lie and listen
Till you can borrow
A few quick beats of a woodpigeon's heart—then rise
See the morning sun on the shaken iris glisten
And say that this home, this valley is wider than Paradise. 20

I have learned it all from my Eve,
This warm dumb wisdom,
She's a finer instructor than years,
She has shown me the strands that weave
Us all one in laughter and tears.   25

I didn't learn it from her speech—
Staggering words:
I can't tell how it comes
But I think the kisses reach
Down where the live web hums.   30

A

Renascence

We have bit no forbidden apple,
   Eve and I,
Yet the splashes of day and night
Falling round us, no longer dapple
The same valley with purple and white.   5
This is our own still valley,
   Our Eden, our home;
But day shows it vivid with feeling,
And the pallor of night does not tally
With dark sleep that once covered the ceiling.   10

The little red heifer: tonight I looked in her eyes;
   She will calve tomorrow.
Last night, when I went with the lantern, the sow was grab-
      bing her litter
With snarling red jaws; and I heard the cries
Of the new-born, and then, the old owl, then the bats that
      flitter.   15

And I woke to the sound of the wood-pigeon and lay and
      listened
   Till I could borrow
A few quick beats from a wood-pigeon's heart; and when I
      did rise
Saw where morning sun on the shaken iris glistened.
And I knew that home, this valley, was wider than Paradise. 20

I learned it all from my Eve,
   The warm, dumb wisdom;
She's a quicker instructress than years;
She has quickened my pulse to receive
Strange throbs, beyond laughter and tears.   25

So now I know the valley
   Fleshed all like me
With feelings that change and quiver

And clash, and yet seem to tally,
Like all the clash of a river   30
    Moves on to the sea.

C

Violets for the Dead

"Did yer notice that lass, sister, as stood away back
By a head-stone?"—
"Nay, I saw nöwt but th' coffin, an' th' yeller clay, an' 'ow
        th' black
Was blown"—

While th' parson was prayin', I watches 'er, an' she wor fair
                shaken   5
To bits"—
"I could think o' nöwt but our Ted, an' 'im taken
In his wild fits."—

"When you'd gone, I slipped back, ter see who she might be—
Poor thing"—   10
"No good, I warrant; this trouble is such as she
Helped to bring."

"You should 'a seen her slive up when we'd go
You should 'a seen her kneel an' look down.
I couldna' see her face, but her little neck shone   15
White, when the wind shifted her hair; that was soft and
                brown,

—An' 'er body fair shook again
Wi' little sobs as you scarce could hear
An' she undid 'er jacket neck, an' then
A lot o' violets fell out of 'er bosom on 'im down theer.   20

"They was wild ones, white and blue;—I could tell
Because they was warm, an' the wind blew

Us a little wift, an' I knew the smell
Then she rummaged her hand in 'er bosom, an' kissed the last
    little few.

"I come away, for fear she should see   25
Me watchin'. Dost think there was öwt between 'em?
Tha knows 'e 'd a winsome way wi 'im, an' she
Was th' little, lovin' sort, as 'as nöwt ter screen 'em."

B

Violets

Sister, tha knows while we was on the planks
    Aside o' th' grave, while th' coffin wor lyin' yet
On th' yaller clay, an' th' white flowers top of it
    Tryin' to keep off 'n him a bit o' th' wet,

An' parson makin' haste, an' a' the black   5
    Huddlin' close together a cause o' th' rain,
Did t' appen ter notice a bit of a lass away back
    By a head-stun, sobbin' an' sobbin' again?

    —How should I be lookin' round
        An' me standin' on the plank   10
    Beside the open ground,
        Where our Ted 'ud soon be sank?

    Yi, an' 'im that young,
        Snapped sudden out of all
    His wickedness, among   15
        Pals worse n'r ony name as you could call.

Let be that; there's some o' th' bad as we
    Like better nor all your good, an' 'e was one.
—An' cos I liked him best, yi, bett'r nor thee,
    I canna bide to think where he is gone.   20

Ah know tha liked 'im bett'r nor me. But let
   Me tell thee about this lass. When you had gone
Ah stopped behind on t' pad i' th' drippin wet
   An' watched what 'er 'ad on.

Tha should ha' seed her slive up when we'd gone,   25
Tha should ha' seed her kneel an' look in
At th' sloppy wet grave—an' 'er little neck shone
   That white, an' 'er shook that much, I'd like to begin

Scraïghtin' my-sen as well. 'En undid her black
   Jacket at th' bosom, an' took from out of it   30
Over a double 'andful of violets, all in a pack
   Ravelled blue and white—warm, for a bit

O' th' smell come waftin' to me. 'Er put 'er face
   Right intil 'em and scraïghted out again,
Then after a bit 'er dropped 'em down that place,   35
   An' I come away, because o' the teemin' rain.

A

Violets

Sister, tha knows while we was on th' planks
   Aside o' t' grave, an' th' coffin set
On th' yaller clay, wi' th' white flowers top of it
   Waitin' ter be buried out o' th' wet?

An' t' parson makin' haste, an' a' t' black   5
   Huddlin' up i' t' rain,
Did t' 'appen ter notice a bit of a lass way back
   Hoverin', lookin' poor an' plain?

   —How should I be lookin' round!
      An' me standin' there on th' plank,   10
      An' our Ted's coffin set on th' ground,
         Waitin' to be sank!

I'd as much as I could do, to think
  Of 'im bein' gone
That young, an' a' the fault of drink   15
  An' carryin's on!—

Let that be; 'appen it worna th' drink, neither,
Nor th' carryin' on as killed 'im.
                          —No, 'appen not,
My sirs! But I say 'twas! For a blither
Lad never stepped, till 'e got in with your lot.—   20

All right, all right, it's my fault! But let
Me tell about that lass. When you'd all gone
Ah stopped behind on t' pad, i' t' pourin' wet
An' watched what 'er 'ad on.

Tha should ha' seed 'er slive up when yer'd gone!   25
Tha should ha' seed 'er kneel an' look in
At th' sloppy grave! an' er' little neck shone
That white, an' 'er cried that much, I'd like to begin

Scraightin' mysen as well. 'Er undid 'er black
Jacket at th' bosom, an' took out   30
Over a double 'andful o' violets, a' in a pack
An' white an' blue in a ravel, like a clout.

An' warm, for th' smell come waftin' to me. 'Er put 'er face
Right in 'em, an' scraighted a bit again,
Then after a bit 'er dropped 'em down that place,   35
An' I come away, acause o' th' teemin' rain.

But I thowt ter mysen, as that wor th' only bit
O' warmth as 'e got down theer; th' rest wor stone cold.
From that bit of a wench's bosom; 'e'd be glad of it,
Gladder nor of thy lilies, if tha maun be told.   40

B

The Piano

Somewhere beneath that piano's superb sleek black
Must hide my mother's piano, little and brown, with the back
That stood close to the wall, and the front's faded silk both
    torn,
And the keys with little hollows, that my mother's fingers had
    worn.

Softly, in the shadows, a woman is singing to me   5
Quietly, through the years I have crept back to see
A child sitting under the piano, in the boom of the shaking
    strings
Pressing the little poised feet of the mother who smiles as she
    sings.

The full throated woman has chosen a winning, living song
And surely the heart that is in me must belong   10
To the old Sunday evenings, when darkness wandered outside
And hymns gleamed on our warm lips, as we watched
    mother's fingers glide.

Or this is my sister at home in the old front room
Singing love's first surprised gladness, alone in the gloom.
She will start when she sees me, and blushing, spread out her
    hands   15
To cover my mouth's raillery, till I'm bound in her shame's
    heart-spun bands

A woman is singing me a wild Hungarian air
And her arms, and her bosom, and the whole of her soul is
    bare,
And the great black piano is clamouring as my mother's never
    could clamour
And my mother's tunes are devoured of this music's ravaging
    glamour.   20

A

The Piano

Softly, in the dusk, a woman is singing to me;
Taking me back down the vista of years, till I see
A child sitting under the piano, in the boom of the tingling
    strings
And pressing the small, poised feet of a mother who smiles
    as she sings.

In spite of myself, the insidious mastery of song   5
Betrays me back, till the heart of me weeps to belong
To the old Sunday evenings at home, with winter outside
And hymns in the cosy parlour, the tinkling piano our guide.

So now it is vain for the singer to burst into clamour
With the great black piano appassionato. The glamour   10
Of childish days is upon me, my manhood is cast
Down in the flood of remembrance, I weep like a child for
    the past.

C

Morality

What a pity, when a man looks at himself in the glass
He doesn't bark at it, like a dog does,
Or fluff up in indignant fury, like a cat!
What a pity he takes himself seriously, and draws a moral
    lesson.

B

Morality

Man alone is immoral
Neither beasts nor flowers are.

Because man, poor beast, can look at himself
And know himself in the glass.

He doesn't bark at himself, as a dog does   5
When he looks at himself in the glass.
He takes himself seriously.

It would be so much nicer if he just barked at himself
Or fluffed up rather angry, as a cat does,
Then turned away and forgot.   10

A

Man's Image

What a pity, when a man looks at himself in a glass
he doesn't bark at himself, like a dog does,
or fluff up in indignant fury, like a cat!

What a pity he sees himself so wonderful,
a little lower than the angels!   5
and so interesting!

D

Glory of Darkness

Blue and dark
Oh Bavarian gentians, tall ones
make a dark-blue gloom
in the sunny room

They have added blueness to blueness, until   5
it is dark: beauty
blue joy of my soul
Bavarian gentians
your dark gloom is so noble!

How deep I have gone   10
dark gentians
since I embarked on your dark blue fringes
how deep, how deep, how happy!
What a journey for my soul
in the dark blue gloom   15
of gentians here in the sunny room!

C

Glory of Darkness

                              . . . .

it is dark
and the door is open
to the depths

it is so blue, it is so dark
in the dark doorway   5
and the way is open
to Hades.

Oh, I know—
Persephone has just gone back
down the thickening thickening gloom   10
of dark-blue gentians to Pluto
to her bridegroom in the dark
and all the dead
and all the dark great ones of the underworld
down there, down there   15
down the blue depths of mountain gentian flowers
cold, cold
are gathering to a wedding in the [winter] dark
down the dark blue path

What a dark-blue gloom   20
of gentians here in the sunny room!

B

Bavarian Gentians

Not every man has gentians in his house
In soft September, at slow, sad Michaelmas.
Bavarian gentians, tall and dark, but dark
darkening the daytime torch-like with the smoking blueness
        of Pluto's gloom,
ribbed hellish flowers erect, with their blaze of darkness
        spread blue,   5
blown flat into points, by the heavy white draught of the day.

Torch-flowers of the blue-smoking darkness, Pluto's dark-blue
        blaze
black lamps from the halls of Dis, smoking dark blue
giving off darkness, blue darkness, upon Demeter's yellow-
        pale day
whom have you come for, here in the white-cast day?   10

Reach me a gentian, give me a torch!
let me guide myself with the blue, forked torch of a flower
down the darker and darker stairs, where blue is darkened on
        blueness
down the way Persephone goes, just now, in first-frosted
        September.
to the sightless realm where darkness is married to dark   15
and Persephone herself is but a voice, as a bride,
a gloom invisible enfolded in the deeper dark
of the arms of Pluto as he ravishes her once again
and pierces her once more with his passion of the utter dark
among the splendour of black-blue torches, shedding fathom-
    less darkness on the nuptials.   20

Give me a flower on a tall stem, and three dark flames,
for I will go to the wedding, and be wedding-guest
at the marriage of the living dark.

$\mathcal{A}$

Bavarian Gentians

Not every man has gentians in his house
in Soft September, at slow, sad Michaelmas.

Bavarian gentians, big and dark, only dark
darkening the day-time, torch-like with the smoking blueness
    of Pluto's gloom,
ribbed and torch-like, with their blaze of darkness spread
    blue   5
down flattening into points, flattened under the sweep of
    white day
torch-flower of the blue-smoking darkness, Pluto's dark-blue
    daze,
black lamps from the halls of Dis, burning dark blue,
giving off darkness, blue darkness, as Demeter's pale lamps
    give off light,
lead me then, lead the way.   10

Reach me a gentian, give me a torch!
let me guide myself with the blue, forked torch of this flower
down the darker and darker stairs, where blue is darkened on
    blueness
even where Persephone goes, just now, from the frosted Sep-
    tember
to the sightless realm where darkness is awake upon the
    dark   15
and Persephone herself is but a voice
or a darkness invisible enfolded in the deeper dark
of the arms Plutonic, and pierced with the passion of dense
    gloom,
among the splendour of torches of darkness, shedding dark-
    ness on the lost bride and her groom.

MARIANNE MOORE

1887–

In 1967, when Miss Moore, the grande dame of American poetry, issued a new edition of her *Complete Poems*, the famous poem "Poetry" received a startling revision. For reasons unknown to the reader, the poetess decided to write a new poem out of her old one. Though this final version contains the very language of the 1921 poem, and represents its tone and point of view, a totally new experience is received as a result of the new concision. Here it is hardly a matter of which poem is better or pleases most; we must accept (or reject) each version as a separate expression or perception. One may question the value of the material left out and the many reasons that may have prompted Miss Moore to re-create her poem. Also, we cannot rule out a "sense of play." After all, this is at the heart of the earlier poem in the first place.

B

Poetry

I, too, dislike it: there are things that are important beyond all this fiddle.
      Reading it, however, with a perfect contempt for it, one
      discovers in it after all, a place for the genuine.
            Hands that can grasp, eyes
            that can dilate, hair that can rise   5
                  if it must, these things are important not be-
                  cause a

high-sounding interpretation can be put upon them but because they are
      useful. When they become so derivative as to become un-

intelligible, the same thing may be said for all of us, that we
>   do not admire what   10
>   we cannot understand: the bat
>   holding on upside down or in quest of some-
>   thing to

eat, elephants pushing, a wild horse taking a roll, a tireless wolf under
>   a tree, the immovable critic twitching his skin like a horse
>   that feels a flea, the base-
>   ball fan, the statistician—   15
>   nor is it valid
>   to discriminate against "business documents and

school-books"; all these phenomena are important. One must make a distinction
>   however: when dragged into prominence by half poets,
>   the result is not poetry,
>   nor till the poets among us can be   20
>   "literalists of
>   the imagination"—above
>   insolence and triviality and can present

for inspection, "imaginary gardens with real toads in them," shall we have
>   it. In the meantime, if you demand on the one hand,   25
>   the raw material of poetry in
>   all its rawness and
>   that which is on the other hand
>   genuine, you are interested in poetry.

Collected Poems, 1963

I, too, dislike it.

$\mathcal{A}$

Poetry

I, too, dislike it.
   Reading it, however, with a perfect contempt for it, one dis-
   covers in
   it, after all, a place for the genuine.

   The Complete Poems of Marianne Moore, 1967

Appendix

TRANSLATIONS

This group of translations, while departing from the general procedure of the text, provides a further example of the way the content and the effect of poetry is determined by shifts in language. We have noted throughout how with slight shifts in words, phrasing, and rhythm, the subject or theme of a poem is altered. The vision of a poem is often changed as a result of minor changes in language. A close examination of these various translations will extend the discipline already learned in the body of this book. There is no need here to examine the original poem—what is important is the way different poets make separate poems out of a single experience. Here the experience is actually someone else's poem. While two translations resemble the original in many aspects, each poem is to be regarded as an independent work, manifesting those very same qualities we find in original works of poetry.

Psalm 15: A Psalm of David

Lord, who shall sojourn in Thy tabernacle?
Who shall dwell upon Thy holy mountain?
He that walketh uprightly, and worketh righteousness,
And speaketh truth in his heart;
That hath no slander upon his tongue,   5
Nor doeth evil to his fellow,
Nor taketh up a reproach against his neighbour;
In whose eyes a vile person is despised,
But he honoureth them that fear the Lord;
He that sweareth to his own hurt,   10
    And changeth not;
He that putteth not out his money on interest,
Nor taketh a bribe against the innocent.
He that doeth these things shall never be moved.

> The Holy Scriptures according to the Masoretic Text (1917)

A Psalm of David: 15

O LORD, who shall sojourn in thy tent?
    Who shall dwell on thy holy hill?
He who walks blamelessly, and does what is right,
    and speaks truth from his heart;
Who does not slander with his tongue,
    and does no evil to his friend, nor takes
    up a reproach against his neighbor;
in whose eyes a reprobate is despised,
    but who honors those who fear the LORD;
Who swears to his own hurt and does not change;
Who does not put out his money at interest,
    and does not take a bribe against the innocent.
He who does these things shall never be moved.

The Holy Bible, Revised Standard Version (1952)

Psalm 15

Lord who shall abide in thy tabernacle? Who shall dwell in
    thy holy hill?
He that walketh uprightly, and worketh righteousness, and
    speaketh the truth in his heart.
He *that* backbiteth not with his tongue, nor doeth evil to his
    neighbor, nor taketh up a reproach against his
    neighbor.
In whose eyes a vile person is contemned; but he honoureth
    them that fear the LORD. *He that* sweareth to *his
    own* hurt, and changeth not.
He that putteth not out his money to usury, nor taketh reward
    against the innocent. He that doeth these *things*
    shall never be moved.

The Holy Bible, King James Version (1611)

✢

When we were come unto the sea-side, where
    Our ship lay, which we shov'd into the deep;
We rear our mast, pull up our sails, and bear
    Aboard with us one male, one female sheep.
And so for Hell we stood, with fears in mind,   5
    And tears in eye. But the fair Circe sent,
To bear us company, a good fore-wind
    That kept our sails full all the way we went.
To winds and steerage we our way commend,
    And careless sit from morning till 'twas dark;   10
Then found ourselves at th' Ocean's farthest end,
    Where up to land the wind had forc'd our bark.

      Homer, *Odyssey* XI, fragment translated by Thomas
      Hobbes (1673)

Arrived now at our ship, we launched, and set
Our mast up, put forth sail, and in did get
Our late-got cattle. Up our sails, we went,
My wayward fellows mourning now th' event,
A good companion yet, a foreright wind   5
Circe (the excellent utterer of her mind)
Supplied our murmuring consorts with, that was
Both speed and guide to our adventurous pass.
All day our sails stood to the winds, and made
Our voyage prosperous. Sun then set, and shade   10
All ways obscuring, on the bounds we fell
Of deep oceanus, where people dwell
Whom a perpetual cloud obscures outright,
To whom the cheerful sun lends never light;
Nor when he mounts the star-sustaining heaven,   15
Nor when he stoops to earth, and sets up Even,
But night holds fix'd wings, feather'd all with banes
Above those most unblest Cimmerians.

      Homer, *Odyssey* XI, fragment translated by George
      Chapman (1616)

But the first that drew anigh me was our friend Elpenor's
      shade
For as yet he was not buried beneath the Earth wide-wayed;
We had left his body unburied, unwept, in Circe's hall,
Since other need and labour on our fellowship did fall.
So I wept when I beheld him and was sorry for his sake,   5
And I sent my voice unto him and a wingèd word I spake:
"How camest thou, Elpenor, beneath the dusk and the dark?
And swifter afoot has thou wended than I in my coal-black
      bark."
God's doom and wine unstinted on me the bane had brought
I lay in the house of Circe and waking had no thought   10
To get me back and adown by the way of the ladders tall:
But downright from the roof I tumbled, and brake my neck
      withal
From the backbone, and unto Hades and his house my soul
      must fare.

> Homer, *Odyssey* XI, fragment translated by William
> Morris (1897)

First came my soldier Elpenor's spirit
    Which left the body just when we set sail,
So that we had no leisure to inter it;
    His heavy fate I did with tears bewail.
How now, quoth I, Elpenor? art thou here   5
    Already? Couldst thou me so much outstrip?
I first came forth, and left thee in the rear
    Hast thou on foot outgone my good black ship?
Then said Elpenor: Issue of Jove, divine
    Ulysses, I had come along with th' bark,   10
But the Devil and excess of wine
    Made me to fall, and break my neck i' th' dark.
I went to bed late by a ladder steep
    At top o' th' house the room was where I lay,
Wak'd at the noise of party, half asleep,   15
    Headlong I hither came, the nearest way.

> Homer, *Odyssey* XI, fragment translated by Thomas
> Hobbes (c.1673–1677)

✣

Caeli, Lesbia nostra

My Lesbia, *that* Lesbia, whom alone Catullus loved
More than himself and all who are most dear to him,
Now in cross-roads and alleys trading her charms
Fleeces the lordly descendants of Remus.

> Catullus, Poem LVIII, translated by R. C. Trevelyan

Caelius, my Lesbia, that one, that only Lesbia,
Lesbia whom Catullus loved more than himself and all things
he ever owned or treasured.
Now her body's given up in alley-ways,
on highroads to these fine Roman gentlemen,
fathered centuries ago by the noble Remus.

> Catullus, Poem LVII, translated by Horace Gregory; from
> *The Poems of Catullus* (1931)

Lesbia me dicit

Lesbia for ever on me rails,
To talk of me, she never fails,
Now, hang me, but for all her art
I find that I have gained her heart.
My proof is this: I plainly see   5
The case is just the same with me;
I cursed her every hour sincerely,
Yet, hang me, but I love her dearly.

> Catullus, Poem XCII, translated by Jonathan Swift

Lesbia, forever spitting fire at me, is never silent. And now
if Lesbia fails to love me, I shall die. Why
do I know in truth her passion burns for me? Because I am
        like her,
because I curse her endlessly. And still, O hear me gods,
I love her.

> Catullus, Poem XCII, translated by Horace Gregory; from
> *The Poems of Catullus* (1931)

The Long Love That in My Thought Doth Harbor

The long love that in my thought doth harbor,
And in my heart doth keep his residence,
Into my face presseth with bold pretense
And there encampeth, spreading his banner.
She that me learns to love and suffer   5
And wills that my trust and lust's negligence
Be reined by reason, shame, and reverence
With his hardiness takes displeasure.
Wherewithal unto the heart's forest he fleeth,
Leaving his enterprise with pain and cry,   10
And there him hideth, and not appeareth.
What may I do, when my master feareth,
But in the field with him to live and die?
For good is the life ending faithfully.

> Petrarch, *Sonetto in Vita* 91, translated by Sir Thomas
> Wyatt the Elder (1557)

Love, That Doth Reign and Live Within My Thought

Love, that doth reign and live within my thought,
And built his seat within my captive breast,
Clad in the arms wherein with me he fought,
Oft in my face he doth his banner rest.
But she that taught me love and suffer pain,   5
My doubtful hope and eke my hot desire
With shamefast look to shadow and refrain,
Her smiling grace converteth straight to ire.
And coward Love, then, to the heart apace
Taketh his flight, where he doth lurk and plain,   10
His purpose lost, and dare not show his face.
For my lord's guilt thus faultless bide I pain,
Yet from my lord shall not my foot remove:
Sweet is the death that taketh end by love.

> Petrarch, *Sonetto in Vita* 91, translated by Henry Howard
> Earl of Surrey (1557)

Hither from her, whence Shame hath sped away,
And Good hath perished in the evil clime,
From Babel, den of dole and dam of crime,
Fleeing I come, to eke my mortal day.
Alone, as Love admonishes, I stray,   5
Culling now flower and herb, now verse and rhyme,
With meditated hope of better time
Cheering my soul, that there alone finds stay.
Fortune and multitude I nothing mind,
Or much myself, or of poor things have heed,   10
Or burn with outer or with inner heat.
Two souls alone I crave, and would indeed
For her, more gentle mood toward me inclined;
For him, his proved stability of feet.

      Petrarch, *Sonetto in Vita* 91, translated by Richard
      Garnett (1835–1906)